Bama, Bear Bryant and the Bible

Bama, Bear Bryant and the Bible

�֍

100 DEVOTIONALS BASED ON THE LIFE OF PAUL "BEAR" BRYANT

David Shepard

Writers Club Press
New York Lincoln Shanghai

Bama, Bear Bryant and the Bible
100 DEVOTIONALS BASED ON THE LIFE OF PAUL "BEAR" BRYANT

Writers Club Press
an imprint of iUniverse, Inc.

For information address:
iUniverse, Inc.
2021 Pine Lake Road, Suite 100
Lincoln, NE 68512
www.iuniverse.com

ISBN: 0-595-25599-X

Printed in the United States of America

To my parents for taking me to church every Sunday morning and Sunday night after the "Bear Bryant Show."

Contents

INTRODUCTION

Why 100 devotionals based on the life of Coach Paul Bryant? The number '100' just happens to be the total number of losses Bear suffered during his football career. That includes playing, being an assistant coach and head coach. Whether we want to admit it or not we seek God's comfort after we have suffered a loss in our lives more than when we are winning. I am sure Coach Bryant sought comfort in the scriptures after a tough loss. Also, Bryant as a head coach played on exactly 100 different dates, from September 9 to January 2.

There are many Christians who think that when God put numbers in the Bible there was no spiritual significance to it, and neither should we apply any meaning to it other than the number itself. But even if we were to look at this issue superficially, we can readily see that there is some method and certain numerical symbol to the use of numbers in scripture. The consistency in their signification in certain situations testifies to this. There is most certainly a great Spiritual defining in the application of many of these numbers. We are often inclined to underestimate God and what He has planted within His Holy Word. There is far more in the scriptures than can be understood in one man's lifetime, and we can only glean the surface of this storehouse of information. For we see through a glass dimly and know only in part.

The Numbers one hundred illustrates the Fullness of whatever is in view, without it "necessarily" being the totality. As a practical illustration, Monday would be a full day, but not the totality of the week. Likewise one hundred would represent the fullness or completeness of that particular day, but not necessarily the totality of the whole week which that day is part of. A perfect Biblical example Luke 15:3-5

*   "And he spoke this parable unto them, saying,
*   What man of you, having an hundred sheep, if he loses one of them, doth not leave the ninety and nine in the wilderness, and go after that which is lost, until he finds it?
*   And when he hath found it, he lays it on his shoulders, rejoicing".

This principle applies. If we lose one of them, we search till we find it. The fullness of them must be found. The number one hundred there signified the fullness of believers, which are shepherded over. It signifies the fullness of whatever is in view, without it necessarily being the totality of it.

FOOTBALL AND RELIGION

In Alabama, there are three classes of people: Alabama Crimson Tide fans, Auburn Tiger fans, and atheists. Two of the three will go to Hades when they die. Which two depends entirely on whom you ask.

Those Alabamians who like football but have no particular team preference are called, "agnostics." It is the hope of the faithful that someday these poor, pathetic souls will purchase an Alabama jacket or be given an Auburn cap and thereby experience the joy of committing themselves to a particular team. Until then, they are considered social and recreational outcasts. To pray for them is all that we can do.

Why all the football references in a column that's supposed to be about religion? Because religion and football are closely entwined, my friend, with much more in common than you may think. Note this passage from the Big Playbook of St. Gipper, recently discovered in a dark basement on the campus of Notre Dame University.

The passage reads: "And on the seventh day God created football and all was right with the world…until Satan brought forth the referees…"

It is impossible to believe in college football without also believing in a Higher Power. Here in Alabama—and in a whole lot of other places—football is a religion. To some, it is the only religion. Blasphemy, you say? I don't think so. More prayers are said and answered during the average college football game than in most churches during a month of Sundays. That explains why evangelists love to hold revivals in football stadiums. The mood has already been set. The congregation holds season tickets.

Consider this: Alabama has been getting a lot of national press lately because of two things: (1) The quality (or lack thereof) of the University of Alabama's football team and (2) Moral stands being taken and legal battles being waged by Alabamians over the separation of church and state. Football and religion. Religion and football. And on we go.

Playing offense for God in Alabama are folks like the high school students who walked out of class because they weren't allowed a moment of prayer before a math test. Personally, I'd rather have my teenagers saying prayers in school classrooms than singing rap songs and riding around in loud cars. I do think these young people are limiting themselves, though. When I was in school we prayed before EVERY test, not just math.

Back to the subject at hand, I think the opinion that football has become a bonafide religion is further attested to by the fact that no one has yet tried to shove a legal crowbar between organized religion and organized college football. Maybe they realize how futile their efforts would be. Or maybe they're just afraid of divine retribution. I understand Bear Bryant was not meant to be crossed while he was here on earth. God forbid some heretic ACLU lawyer upset him now.

When the Universities of Alabama and Auburn play one another, the faithful drop whatever they're doing and flock to the game like wise men chasing a far off star. The entire state stands still. Try finding a washing machine repairman or an emergency room doctor during an Alabama/Auburn game. They are nowhere to be found. You may die in dirty clothes, but that's what you get for not attending the big game.

The ending of the Iron Bowl is of apocalyptic proportions. In the final moments of the game, just before the buzzer sounds to signal the end, everyone's faith is put to the test. As the clock ticks down—6...5...4...3...2...1...you were either devoutly for Alabama or had completely given your life to Auburn. There was no "Atheist" section in these stands.

Every fall weekend thousands of students and alumni here drape themselves in sacred colors (crimson and white), bear on their bodies images of their religious totem (elephants), snake across the Southeast in long pilgrimage lines (RVs), in their journey to houses of worship (football stadiums), where they sing hymns ("Yea Alabama"), drone chants ("Defense, Defense") and participate in rituals (Ramma Jamma cheer) in worship of their saint-like team (Crimson Tide) and super human coach (Bear Bryant).

At Notre Dame, the "Touchdown Jesus" mural high on the library behind the stadium seems to bless every Irish passage into end zone heaven. Is football a religion?

Sociologists tell us that every community must have some sort of religion that organizes and reinforces the purpose of its members. In essence, football's sacred pageantry and rituals appear to act as a religion for many colleges and universities. People come together from all walks of life on a Saturday afternoon to participate in a kind of religious experience that affirms their common bond as members of the same college tribe.

But let's not take this too far. Unless we take such bumper sticker lines as "Alabamian by Birth, Crimson Tide by the Grace of God" as somehow profoundly meaningful, the religion of football offers precious few explanations for life's purpose and meaning. Following Bear Bryant cannot easily be confused with following Christ. Can it?

I'm drawing this analogy between football and religion partly because it's fun and partly because it demonstrates the work the church today. Its purpose is to preach to fans and convert them. They take as their task a willingness to enter into conversation with fans about fundamental questions of meaning and value in our lives.

You know it used to be that the only education was religious education. All of the great private universities in this country—Harvard, Yale and all—began as colonial era colleges for training young men for the ministry. In fact, as late as the Civil War, the president of every college in this country was a moral philosopher whose primary teaching role was to verse the senior class in what it might mean to lead a good and moral life.

Those days have passed. With the rise of science in the latter part of the nineteenth century and the burgeoning of knowledge, religion—once the core of the curriculum—was shunted further and further into the background.

Alabama is one of the few places in the country where the wearing of crimson and white together is encouraged. We do this, I think, to affirm our common bonds as people of this place, this university, but also I would hope, to affirm our common commitment to the highest ideals of what it might mean to be a good person, a responsible citizen in a changing society.

ACCOUNTABILTY

o o o o o o o o o o o o o o o o o o o o o o o o o o o o o o o o
"To judge everyone, and to convict all the ungodly of all the
ungodly acts they have done in the ungodly way, and of all
the harsh words ungodly sinners have spoken against him.
These men are grumblers and faultfinders; they follow their
own evil desires; they boast about themselves and flatter others for their own advantage. But, dear friends, remember
what the apostles of our Lord Jesus Christ foretold." Jude
1:15-17

This is what happened at Birmingham's Legion Field on Dec. 2, 1972:
Alabama was undefeated, untied and ranked second in the nation.
Auburn, had forged a surprising 8–1 record and were ranked ninth
nationally. Still, a 35–7 loss to LSU marred their record, and they were
16-point underdogs to the Tide. With 5:30 to play, the score 16–3 and
the ball at midfield, Auburn linebacker Bill Newton rushed through
unchecked and blocked Greg Gantt's punt. The ball took a perfect hop
into the arms of defensive back David Langner, who sped 25 yards into
the end zone. Jett's extra point made it 16–10. Then, with 1:34
remaining, Gantt prepared to punt again. The line of scrimmage was
the Alabama 43. And again, Newton blocked Gantt's punt. It bounded
as if by design into Langner's arms, and he returned it 20 yards for the
touchdown with 1:24 remaining. Jett's PAT gave Auburn a most
improbable 17–16 victory. Bear took the blame for the mistakes.

Accountability is something most of us do not like to think about.
To be accountable means one has to be responsible for one's actions
and choices. God's Word is very clear: everyone will be held account-

able for choices made and actions taken on this earth. The ultimate accountability will be the choice one makes with God's most precious gift to us in Jesus. As one makes Jesus the Savior and Lord of their life they then become accountable for what they do for Jesus. God equips each of His children to make an impact for Him in the "world" in which they are placed. One day every child of God will give an account of how their life was spent and how they allowed God to be glorified in and through their life. As God's children become aware of what God expects they can become more sensitive and determined to please Him in making their life count for eternal significance.

"A bad practice, a bad game, it's up to the head coach to assume his responsibility."

—Paul "Bear" Bryant

AGONIZING OVER DECISIONS

○ ○
"A being in agony he prayed more earnestly." Luke 22:44

Bud Wilkinson gladly opened the vault for Bryant in spite of the fact that his Kentucky Wildcats had ended Oklahoma's 31-game winning streak on a cold and windy afternoon at the Sugar Bowl in New Orleans. For days leading to the game, Bryant had agonized over the Split-T offense that provided huge running lanes for All-America back Billy Vessels and Leon Heath. Finally, he decided to scrap his three-man defensive line in favor of a five-man line. He also moved the defensive backs three yards closer to the line of scrimmage, daring quarterback Claude Arnold to beat the Wildcats with his arm. Arnold had a rough day and Kentucky's Babe Parilli threw two touchdown passes to Shorty Jamerson and the Wildcats pulled off a monumental upset 13-7.

In 1968, Admiral Elmo Zumwalt Jr. took command of the American naval forces in Vietnam. In an effort to reduce US casualties, he ordered the waterways sprayed with the chemical defoliant Agent Orange. It was a move designed to push back the jungle and make it harder for North Vietnamese to ambush Navy river patrol boats at point-blank range. One of those boats was commanded by his 21-year-old son, Lieutenant Elmo Zumwalt III, who died of cancer in 1988. The admiral believed that Agent Orange killed his son. What a heart-breaking story of a father who made a decision that resulted in great suffering for his own son! How much greater was the heartbreak of

God the Father when He provided salvation for us! He made a decision that resulted in immeasurable agony for His only Son. Think of how God must have felt as He watched His Son suffer the mockery of the crowd, the lashes of the whip, the pain of the nails through His hands and feet, the inexpressible weight and humiliation of our sins, and the indescribable agony of isolation and abandonment.

Father, forgive us for adding to your pain by our lack of gratitude. Please help us to live in a way that will honor Your Son, who defeated sin and death—for us

> "If you start to make a decision, go ahead and make it. Don't mealy mouth around."
>
> —Bear Bryant

ALL STAR

○ ○
"When I consider your heavens, the work of your fingers, the moon and the stars, which you have set in place" Psalm 8:3

Bear Bryant soon made all-star on a very talented football team that won the state championship in 1930. In fact, one of Fordyce's opponents was Pine Bluff High, which featured a superb end named Don Hudson. He was also named to the All-American team and Silver Anniversary All-American team. He was inducted into the National Football foundation College Football Hall of Fame in 1986, the Alabama Sports Hall of fame in 1969, Arkansas Hall of Fame in 1964, national Coach of the year 1961, 1971,1973, SEC Coach of the century, SEC Coach of the year, 1950, 1961, 1964, 1965, 1971, 1973, 1974, 1977, 1979 and 1981 and was presented the Presidential Medal of Freedom, 1983.

Bear Bryant had 80 players named to the All-American team and 158 named to All-Conference teams.

Christians are so accustomed to reading through the Old Testament without applying what it says that they miss this link between God and the stars. This passage, first of all, tells believers to look to the heavens for a statement about God Himself. Isaiah's evidence is the stars. First, he says, God created the stars. Second, God calls them forth in an orderly system. Third, God calls them by names that denote the power of His might. In other words, the names of the stars are given by God, and the names of the stars are each unique, meaningful descriptors of God's might. And fourth, because God is sovereign, not one star fails to be proved out. In other words, God names each of them with a declaration of His power, and because He is so powerful, each star and its declaration is proved (i.e., "not one fails").

"I was in awe of all the movie stars at the Rose Bowl."

—Bear Bryant

ANGER

"The LORD is slow to anger, and great in power, and will not at all acquit the wicked: the LORD hath his way in the whirlwind and in the storm, and the clouds are the dust of his feet." Nahum 1:3

John David Crow didn't know who Coach Bryant was at the time, he was just a country boy up there, but he knew Coach Elmer and his mother and father trusted Coach Elmer, and when he said this would be the best place for him to come, that was pretty much it." Although Crow didn't know who Bryant was at the time, it didn't take long for Bryant to make a name for himself. And as someone on the inside, Crow has vivid memories of the man they called "Bear." "It's very difficult to put the feel and the taste of the time there, because Coach Bryant was a tough person and I'll admit that, he was very, very demanding," Crow said. "But he was fair and he was just. He had feelings, he was not a man that was afraid to show his emotions not only with anger or disappointment, but also with kindness and caring and his showing of tears and choking up.

"He was that kind of person. Therefore you can tell that he was my favorite person, possibly outside of my father."

The notion that Christians should not be angry, or that anger is inappropriate, is irrational and unbiblical. Have you considered how Jesus responded when the Pharisees discounted Him and His teaching? The same way He reacted when the moneychangers discounted the sanctity of the temple. He got really mad. He lashed out, spoke harshly, turned over tables, and cracked His whip on people's backs until He had satisfied His anger!

If Jesus Christ exhibited anger, then anger cannot be sin. But Scripture does not end with the imperative to be angry. We are to be angry, but we are not to sin in the process.

There must be an inherent danger associated with being angry and sinning. If this were not a real possibility, God would not counsel us as He does in Scripture.

When does anger become sin? Anger becomes sin when you hold onto it as if it belongs to you. It does not!

"Don't talk after a game until you cool off."

—Bear Bryant

APOLOGIZING

o o o o o o o o o o o o o o o o o o o o o o o o o o o o o o o

"Confess your faults one to another, and pray for each other, that you may be healed. The effectual fervent prayer of a righteous man avails much." James 5:16

The players were mad when Bear Bryant left Maryland. He got the Kentucky job, and he was gone in a flash. Maryland got a Gator Bowl invitation and couldn't accept it because they didn't have anyone to coach them.

Many times through the years Coach Bryant apologized to the Maryland players for leaving like he did. He felt he had bailed out on them. He had a good reason to leave, but he was never comfortable thinking he had reneged on a commitment. On the morning he was to break Stagg's record for wins, he was still apologizing.

The Arizona Republic recently carried the story of Patrick Poland, who had been convicted of murder. The day before his execution, Poland said, "I want to say I'm sorry. I've lived with this every day and I wish I could go back in time and correct what was done. I hope every one can accept my apology, understand me, and forgive me." But, despite Poland's remorse and passionate plea to spare his life, the Arizona Board of Executive Clemency voted 4 to 1 to go ahead with Poland's execution. He died by lethal injection the next day.

Both stories send a strong message that apologizing is not the same as repenting. We can be ever so apologetic about our sins, and not be repentant. The Bible teaches that without repentance there is no forgiveness. Let's pursue this thought further.

"Always be totally loyal to the institution for which you work. If you don't have the best interest of the organization at heart or if you cant be loyal, you are in the wrong place."

—Bear Bryant

AWE

o o o o o o o o o o o o o o o o o o o o o o o o o o o o o o o

"Therefore, since we are receiving a kingdom that cannot be shaken, let us be thankful, and so worship God acceptably with reverence and awe." Hebrews 12:28

Bear Bryant said, "I'm not worried about whether I'm going to win or lose. I know I'm going to win. I know that. And I'm not worried about my assistant coaches. I know they're winners. And I'm not worried about whether Alabama is going to win. I know that. The only thing I don't know is how many of you in this room are winners, and how many of you will be with us."

Bryant said that he'd be back after the bowl game with Texas A&M and that when he got back, they were going to work—and those who were winners would be around to see the rewards, and those who weren't, wouldn't. The players were in awe of him. In fact, they were scared to death of him.

I stand in awe of God and His holiness. And because I do, I love Him and want to be close to Him. I desire to love what He loves and hate what He hates. I want to live with the awareness that He is to be feared more than anyone. Yes, I admit I'm afraid of God. I also fear water. That doesn't mean I don't like to swim or fish. But I can never forget the life-taking power of a lake or an ocean. The same is true in my relationship with God. I respect His authority as my heavenly father. Only as we fear God do we truly love Him. And only as that love grows will it guarantee that our fear of God is the right kind of fear.

"I am nervous around a lot of people, in awe of what they have accomplished."

—Bear Bryant

BRITCHES

o o o o o o o o o o o o o o o o o o o o o o o o o o o o o o o o
"Stand therefore, having girded you waist with truth" Ephesians 6:14

His assistant coaches gave Bear Bryant the nickname "Britches". Several of the coaches were in the dressing room talking when someone asked why they did a certain thing a certain way. Coach Bryant wasn't there at the time, of course, but his locker was open and his khaki pants were hanging in full view. Pat James pointed to those pants and said," I'm going to do whatever the guy who wears those britches says." He was never called that to his face and it is not sure if he ever knew it.

When Bill's mother reminded him that he hadn't studied his Sunday school lesson or learned the memory verse, he looked up from his work on an airplane model. "Aw, Mom, I know all that stuff," he argued. "I don't need to study. I go to church and Sunday school, to Boys' Club, and even to a Christian school." But when Dad gave him a stern look, he obediently worked on his lesson until bedtime. The following morning when Mother told Bill to get ready for church, he protested that he already knew "all that stuff the pastor says." Unwillingly, he went to his room to change, but in a few minutes was back again. "Look at these pants!" he exclaimed. "They're getting awful short on me." Mom nodded. "So they are," she agreed. "You've grown right out of them. We'll look for a new pair this week." Good idea," approved Dad, who was listening. He grinned. "I guess those pants must have shrunk," he said, "or could it be that you're growing up?" Then he became serious. "But, Bill, I'm concerned, because lately I get the feeling that you think God is like that old pair of pants." Bill looked at

Dad. "What do you mean?" he asked." Well, you've implied that you know all there is to know about God," explained Dad. "You seem to think you've outgrown Him. Actually, you'll need a whole lifetime to learn about God and His Word, and then you'll still know only just a little. God is so great and so wonderful, we'll never know all there is to know." That's right," said Mom. "That's something you ought to remember while you're sitting in church this morning…and when it's time to do your Sunday school lesson and learn Bible verses, too." Bill looked down at the short pants he was wearing. "Okay. I'll remember," he promised. "I get the point!" And sure enough…as he thought about the words of the songs and as he listened to the pastor and Sunday school teacher that morning, he heard several things he hadn't known before.

> *"When we moved to Fordyce, Mama bought me some khaki britches."*
>
> —Bear Bryant

BROKEN BONES

"Make me to hear joy and gladness; that the bones which thou hast broken may rejoice." Psalms 51:8

Bryant was a good football player, but was always overshadowed by the legendary Don Hutson, his former high school rival. He was known as "the opposite end" but earned a reputation as a tough player.

During a game against Tennessee in 1935, Bryant would display the iron resolution that would become his trademark in years to come by playing with a broken leg. Bryant was magnificent in a 25-0 victory. An Atlanta paper doubting the veracity of the report of the fractured bone requested x-rays to impugn the credibility of the Tide medical staff. The x-rays proved without question, the end named Bear Bryant had indeed competed in an agonizing situation, and had the game of his career.

God, in favor to his children, does afflict them for sin; and the very phrase of breaking his bones, though it express extremity of misery and pain, yet it hath hope in it, for broken bones by a cunning hand may be set again and return to their former use and strength; so that a conscience distressed for sins is not out of hope; yet upon that hope no wise man will adventure upon sin, saying, though I am wounded, yet I may be healed again; though I am broken, I may be repaired; for let him consider who breaks his bones—Thou; he that made us our bones and put them in their several places, and tied them together with ligaments, and covered them with flesh; he that keeps all our bones from breaking; it must be a great matter that must move him to break the bones of any of us. The God of all consolation, that comforts us in all our distresses, when he cometh to distress us, this makes affliction weigh heavy bring it in subjection, even to the crucifying of the flesh with the lusts thereof. Therefore, let no man adventure his bones in hope of setting them again.

"Is there any chance of a bone sticking out anywhere?"
—Bear Bryant asking Dr. Sherrill before the Tennessee game

BUSINESS

∘ ∘

"When his parents saw him, they were astonished, and his mother said to him, "Son, why have you done this to us? Your father and I have been looking for you with great anxiety." And he said to them, "Why were you looking for me? Did you not know that I must be about my Father's business?" Luke 2:48-49

One of Alabama's best players showed up late and was locked out. He started pounding on the door, trying to get in. Coach Bryant turned to his assistant coach and said, "Go see who that is. And tell him, whoever it is, that we don't need him." The team learned right then and there that Bear meant business.

Have you been about your Fathers business this week? Has God had a good laugh on your behalf because you tried to be loving and gracious like you heavenly father? You may not have been very effective, but did you try? Did you learn by modeling God? Did you develop skills that your Father may want you to use later?

This week, did you seek out your place in God's plan? Did you try to discover who you were as a child of God? A child learns their place in a family or society by interacting with others. In your day-to-day activities did you practice being a member of the family of God? Sometimes discovering what your place is in the world is hard, but did you try.

For three days Jesus was in his fathers house and was about his father's business. He asked and answered questions and imitated his father and sought out his identity. "And Jesus grew in wisdom and in stature, and in favor with God and humankind." And God was over-joyed. When we do the same, we will grow, and God the Father can't help but smile on us.

> *"We decided to pool our resources and become business tycoons. We bought a cleaning and pressing place called the Captain Kidd Cleaners."*

—Bear Bryant

THE CHALLENGE OF CHANGE

○ ○
"You saw me before I was born and scheduled each day of my life before I began to breathe. Every day was recorded in your book." Psalms 139:16

Another disappointing season in 1970 saw the Tide go 6-5-1. Many critics and fans were left wondering if Bryant's magical touch had aged beyond repair. Bryant himself wondered if the college game had passed him by, considering retirement and even entertaining offers from NFL. He knew he had to do something drastic to turn the fortunes of the Tide and secure his legacy at Alabama.

Does God really know what I'm going through? Is He really aware that things are changing so rapidly? When God said each day was scheduled, didn't He mean that I would graduate from school, get a job, stay there for 40 years, get a gold watch and retire? How could God have known that my jobs would last an average of 3.2 years, and thereby I would have 14-16 different jobs in my working career? If you were called to a particular field or position, how does unwelcome change fit in? It is critical that a person has a clear sense of purpose and calling in today's changing world. If we don't know our Purpose in life, any obstacle will send us in a new direction. Life is never made unbearable by circumstances, but only by lack of meaning and purpose. Knowing our purpose allows us to respond to make new decisions based on our priorities and values, rather than on circumstances. The only way we can tolerate the rapid change today is to know what is changeless about us. With so many options, it's easy to get off track or misdirect.

Change, while not welcomed, often is prodding a person to a higher level of success. The Eagle nest—the eaglets are forced to move out of the nest, not to crash to the ground, but to learn to fly!!

Is change impacting your profession—your calling??

"A lot of things were going on in those days, and I did a poor job of coping. If I hadn't been so busy going off in all directions things would have been better."

—Bear Bryant

CHANGE

o o o o o o o o o o o o o o o o o o o o o o o o o o o o o o o
"Behold, I show you a mystery; we shall not all sleep, but we shall all be changed," 1Corinthians 15:51

Bryant was on his way to Jacksonville where Texas A&M was playing in the Gator Bowl, when he came to Tuscaloosa to meet the football team. The players had heard how tough he was, and how things were going to change. They soon learned after he called a team meeting at the dorm and sent out word for everybody to be there at 1:15 in the afternoon.

Yes, it is true that God is the same yesterday, today, and forever.

The prophet Malachi wrote, "For I, Jehovah, change not..." (3:6). And in Hebrews 13:8, the inspired penman writes, "Jesus Christ is the same yesterday and to-day, yea and for ever."

So it is clear that God doesn't change. He is Deity. And those characteristics, which establish his divinity, will never change.

But regarding whether the Lord works miraculously today or not, please think about these things.

While God doesn't change, his activity in the affairs of people may—and occasionally has

Although he changes not, his interaction with humanity, as determined by his sovereign will, has changed throughout history.

The first woman was formed in a special way, by a miracle (Genesis 2:18-23). Jehovah took a bone and some flesh from Adam and fashioned a beautiful helper, suitable for the man. Many of us today have wives—yet we still have all our ribs!

God is still the same, is he not? Yes. But he is Lord, and he operates in his universe as he pleases—consistent with his will.

> *"Formations don't win football games, people do. But they can give you an edge and that's what coaches look for. That is why we change so much."*
>
> —Bear Bryant

CHARISMA

○ ○
"Charisma is deceitful and beauty is vain, but a person who fears the Lord, shall be praised." Proverbs 31:30

Bear Bryant had something nobody else has had. Certain people have that something special—call it charisma—but he had it. Before you saw him, you knew he was in a room because when he came in you could hear a pin drop. He dominated a room, a football stadium or wherever he was. He was an absolutely a unique person, and there will never be another like him.

One of the words which has come into wide use (actually misuse) in our generation is the word "charisma," along with its derivative "charismatic." We speak of a politician as having charisma, or a charismatic personality, for example. Another common use of "charismatic" refers to those who practice speaking in tongues. But these are not the true meanings of these words, at least not in terms of their original usage.

This latter usage, in particular, comes from the inclusion of tongues as one of the "gifts" of the Holy Spirit. The Greek word is charisma. It does not mean "tongues," and neither does it mean an outgoing and articulate manner. It simply means "gift," or better, "free gift," a classic example being Romans 6:23: "The gift of God is eternal life through Jesus Christ our Lord."

Charisma, in turn, comes from Charis, which means "grace," and is usually so translated. For example, in the words of our text, if the "word of Christ dwells in us richly," we shall be "singing with grace in our hearts." Furthermore, just a few verses further on, we are admonished to "Let your speech be always with grace" (Colossians 4:6). Then,

Paul concludes the Colossian epistle with: "Grace be with you. Amen" (Colossians 4:18).

Thus, true grace in our hearts will produce grace in our speech, and the grace of the Lord Jesus Christ will always be with us! This is the true charisma! A truly charismatic person is a gracious person—one to whom "God is able to make all grace abound" so that he or she, "always having all sufficiency in all things, may abound to every good work"

"I don't know what charisma is, but I can tell when one has it. You can tell it from a mile away."

—Bear Bryant

CONFIDENCE

o o o o o o o o o o o o o o o o o o o o o o o o o o o o o o o o
"Cast not away therefore your confidence, which hath great recompense of reward." Hebrews 10:35

Of his childhood, Bryant said, "The one thing I disliked most about growing up was getting up every Saturday, hitching up our mule to our wagon and going to Fordyce with Mama. I didn't mind the work. In fact, I'd love to be with Mama again doing that today. What I hated about it was coming face-to-face with the people we met along the way. I had an inferiority complex. I didn't feel like I was as good as those people. I thought they looked down on me."

Bear was so timid when he first arrived in Fordyce that he would barely talk to anyone. He was a nice looking guy, about six foot tall and extremely handsome, who ended up having a girl in every town. But he was so bashful during those first few months around school with his head down to keep from meeting anybody.

Much of his inspiration and angry determination to succeed in life resulted from those early years as he set out to prove he was as good as anyone.

You see, we are programmed to see ourselves a certain way by the words people speak to us and the experiences of our lives. If the words we hear are positive and our experiences wonderful, then we usually have a good self-image. Obviously, you have experienced the opposite. How can you overcome all these negative words and bad experiences? The answer is all in the Bible. You need to reprogram your mind to God's Word. You must think about yourself the way God thinks about you. And how does God see you? He sees you "in Christ."

"Little things make me proud."

—Bear Bryant

CORRECTING MISTAKES

o o o o o o o o o o o o o o o o o o o o o o o o o o o o o
"Correct your son and he shall give you rest; he will give
delight to your soul." Proverbs 29:16

Coach Bryant would say, "So how did that second period go at practice
yesterday, when we were working on defense?" The assistant coach
would say, "Oh, it was great. Our linebackers were really hitting and
the ends were fantastic." That's when Coach Bryant would let the assistant coach answering the question sweat for a while and say, "You
know that is not right—or you should know. Old' so and so didn't hit
a person and old' so and so was so out of position on most plays he
couldn't have gotten close enough to a runner to even attempt a tackle.
How can they learn anything if you cant see that well enough to correct mistakes?" Coach Bryant didn't miss a thing. He saw it all from his
observation tower.

Experts say one of the biggest traps people fall into is protecting others from the consequences of their mistakes. When we constantly rescue others, they learn dependence and irresponsibility. Not holding
them accountable sends this message: "I tolerate this behavior, so
therefore I approve of it." People need to learn to deal with the results
of their mistakes directly.

When the violation has been major, we should try to reestablish
trust in small steps. As the person behaves responsibly, he can have
more privileges or freedom. Remind people not to impose penalties or
consequences too harsh for the mistake.

Although people are becoming more independent, they still need
guidance, understanding, and lots of support. As you keep tugging

away at your end of the rope, you'll find that these challenges aren't just a time of stress, but also a time of growth for everyone.

> *"If a person doesn't help himself—if he isn't accountable for his own mistakes or oversights—he shouldn't expect others to help him either."*
>
> —Bear Bryant

COWS

"The cow and the bear shall feed; their young ones shall lie down together; and the lion shall eat straw like an ox." Isaiah 11:7

Bear Bryant rarely said anything that would offend or inspire an opposing team, but sometime before the Iron Bowl of 1972, he said something about auburn being a "cow college." Alabama was favored in the game, but auburn blocked tow punts late in the game and won 17-16. His cow college remark didn't have anything to do with auburn winning but he didn't forget it. The following spring, after practice one day, he was talking about how the players had performed and said," We looked like a cow college out there today, change that to barber college."

Michael Blake, a farmer in Western Victoria, Australia for over 40 years. He was describing the behavior of one of his sheep named Hercules. Hercules was abandoned at birth, but adopted by a cow on the farm. The cow supplied Hercules with milk and now Hercules believes he is a calf himself. Hercules only hangs out with the farm's bulls. Call this a parable, allegory, or modern day metaphor, but what we have here is a sheep that lives where it doesn't belong. This is a parable for all of us. We all either are, or have been those who live or have lived where we do or did not belong. Scripture recognizes us as sheep over and over. We are often likened to sheep. In a sense we all are one of two kinds of sheep and metaphorically there are really only two kinds of sheep. One kind of sheep is that which is still lost, the other is one which has been found. The sheep that lives with the cows on the farm in the story we started with is still a lost sheep. There is coming a time when Hercules will be weaned from the cows and put back, where he belongs, into the heard of other sheep. And though many of us are sheep that are now living in the flock of God, we often live like we are not of that fold. There are many times when we act like Hercules and run with the bulls when we really belong with the sheep. The message of the gospel is the we do not need to run with bulls any longer, but rather we may join with and fellowship with those who, like us, have been renewed by grace. We often behave otherwise, and stray like sheep, but the shepherd awaits and eagerly seeks our return to the fold.

> *"Sure I'd love to beat Notre Dame, don't get me wrong. But nothing matters more than beating that cow college on the other side of the state"*
>
> —Bear Bryant.

CURIOSITY

○ ○
"Whatever is sold in the shambles, eat, asking no question for curiosity sake." 1 Corinthians 10:25

"Coach Wilkinson and coach Bryant were always trying to outdo each other, but they were like milk and cereal," Darrell Royal once said. "They just got along better than any two that I knew." Royal should know. As a graduated OU quarterback, he was dispatched by Wilkinson in 1951 to Lexington to teach the Split-T offense to Bryant. Though Wilkinson was the master of the intricate option offense that would produce winning streaks of 31 and 47 games, he was never afraid to share with his friend, even if it meant a 0-2 record against the Bear." That was quite an experience, walking around with the head coach of the University of Kentucky and teaching him our offense," Royal told author Keith Dunnavant in "Coach," his unmatched biography of Bryant. "Coach Bryant had a real curiosity about the game. If somebody had developed something that worked, he wanted to know all about it."

Remember Curious George? This is a monkey who's forever getting in trouble. He lands in jail for calling the fire department. He tries to swipe a balloon and ends up floating across the sky. He spills ink all over the floor, and then floods the house trying to clean it up. He eats a puzzle piece and winds up in the hospital. He breaks his leg trying to escape from irate painters. He feeds a bugle to an ostrich. You'd think George would learn. But time after time his curiosity gets the better of him and he ends up in trouble.

Sound familiar? How many times have you wondered what it would be like to try something you know is wrong? How often have you let sin win and ended up getting in trouble because of it? Everyone struggles with sin, but believers have the answer for that struggle. It's not learning to live a completely sinless life—it's God.

We will eventually be free in heaven. In the meantime, the struggle continues. But through the indwelling of the Holy Spirit, we can still live lives that bring glory to God. Christ is the answer. Through Him and His death and resurrection, we are free from the power of sin. He will rescue you from the draw of sin, from the kind of curiosity that got George in trouble every time.

> *"I guess I just showed you that the big fellers of the SEC are a little tougher than the little fellers from that Big Seven Conference."*
>
> —Bear Bryant, After Kentucky's victory in the 1951 Sugar Bowl

DEFENSE

○ ○

"Sanctify the Lord in your hearts and make a defense to everyone who asks you a reason of the hope that is in you with gentleness and reverence" I Pet. 3:15

Bear Bryant believed in defense first, but his coaching style want necessarily conservative it was intelligent. He was light years ahead of other coaches. He had a good, sound imagination offensively than people ever gave him credit for. He established a reputation as a defensive minded coach because the game was a close perimeter minded game when he came to Alabama, but you have to know a lot about offense to coach defense. He did a great job of planning offensively and defensively because he was six to eight years ahead of everybody else. It seems everything he did was copied in some way later by other coaches.

We must be willing to support and defend our faith in all circumstances, no matter what the cost might be to us or to our well being. Today, many persons in the Christian faith are in the faith because they want their faith to give them well being or pay dividends. In reality, the well being of persons in the faith must often be sacrificed because the darkness wants to kill our faith in Christ. If we are faithful, every day the Lord restores us and makes us new so we can carry on in spite of persecutions by evil and darkness. As part of the persecution we must endure, both Satan and the satanic influences of the world make us old and will consume us until we die. By being faithful, we live in God and God has mercy upon us. God pours out His blessings on us as a result of our willingness to believe in Him, our willingness to stand up for Him, and our willingness to defend Him. When we are faithful to God then God is faithful to us. When we are faithful, God is new every day even when our life seems humdrum and boring. When we are faithful, God does not get old. As we are willing to stand up for God, God is faithful to us and He will stand up for us. As a result of our faith in Him, God will never leave us or forsake us. God is, and remains, infinite. God's faithfulness to us is infinite as well.

> *"I always thought Coach Bryant was a perfect example of contra-diction when it came to strategy. He preached defense and kicking over and over, but he would spend about six hours out of every eight dabbling with the offense."*
>
> —Kirk McNair, Alabama SID

DESTROYING ENEMIES

o o o o o o o o o o o o o o o o o o o o o o o o o o o o o o o o
"And ye shall chase your enemies, and they shall fall before you." Leviticus 26:7

There weren't many prospects for a poor farmer in rural Arkansas and Bear wanted more than anything to get out of Fordyce. One afternoon while in eighth grade, Paul was watching a varsity football practice when the coach walked up to him and asked him if he knew how to play. Paul explained it was the first time he'd ever seen the game. The coach told Paul, "See that man down there with the ball? You just go down there and try to kill him." Bryant knew how to do that, so when he caught the ball, Bear ran down and destroyed the poor safety. The following Friday he was in the starting lineup.

Your natural attitude toward your enemies is likely to be pretty much the same as King David's hard-nosed prayer, Break their teeth in their mouth, O God! (Psalm 58.6) But the Bible teaches you a better way (nay, the ONLY way) for defeating your enemies.

Namely, the Bible's shocking strategy for dealing with your enemies is this…

Destroy them!!!

Moreover, Matthew 5.43-48 deliberately teaches you the two best ways to destroy your enemy! Namely…

*   Love him to death
*   Turn him into your friend

"There was no reason in the world for him to help me. But Coach Bryant had the ability to care about other people."

—Larry Lacewell, Arkansas St. Coach

DISAPPOINTMENT

o o o o o o o o o o o o o o o o o o o o o o o o o o o o o o o
"I am the Lord; those who hope in Me will not be disappointed."—Isaiah 49:23 NIV

After a disappointing '82 season, Paul Bryant announced he was retiring at seasons end. He said the decision had come because he wasn't pleased with himself anymore. "This is my school, my alma mater. I love it and I love my players. But in my opinion they deserved better coaching than they have been getting from me this year."

I doubt a day goes by in your life or mine when someone doesn't disappoint us. A friend fails to call when she said she would. A neighbor forgets to return your rake. A colleague at work overlooks a lunch date with you. A promised delivery never arrives. Or someone fails to live up to your expectations. Your child brings home a poor report card. A friend whose spiritual life you esteem drops out of Bible study. Your spouse doesn't affirm you as often as you'd like. Or you experience rejection. A university turns down your application. A cherished job opportunity doesn't pan out. A relationship fizzles. And there are times when we suffer actual injustice at the hands of others. Your boss blames you for a problem that wasn't your fault. A repairman charges you for work not done. Someone sideswipes your car and drives on. When others let us down, it's normal not only to feel hurt but also to think that our destiny has somehow been thwarted. We fear we've been cheated out of benefits that should rightfully be ours. It's the rare moment of faith when we consider that God may see things differently.

"People ask me how I feel about those people who started the mess about fixing a game? Well how would you feel? They tried to destroy me for a lousy $6000. I am very disappointed."

—Bear Bryant

DISCIPLINE

"My son, do not despise the Lord's discipline and do not resent his rebuke, because the Lord disciplines those he loves, as a father the son he delights in." Proverbs 3:11-12

As a player, Bryant was the prototype of the coach he would become. Head Coach Frank Thomas recognized that and hired him as an assistant coach when his playing days ended. Bryant was just 23 years old. He soon married his college sweetheart and campus beauty, Mary Harmon and the couple would soon have two children. After four successful years as assistant coach, Bryant took a job as Red Sanders' number one assistant at Vanderbilt in 1940. Bryant quickly earned a reputation as a demanding coach and strict disciplinarian

God uses discipline as a last resort. If all God needed to justify mankind to himself was a bigger cattle-prod, then Christ died for nothing! No, God's plan for the earth is love first, discipline last. To get us to listen and repent, he will use deep conviction, the rebuke of friends, coincident sermons, the quickening of Scripture, and every other means before disciplining us. But if we resist God's Spirit of light and mercy, we are promised the rod of correction. When God disciplines, the punishment fits the crime. Time and again, we realize that we cannot get away with unrepentant sin. God is sculpting us into holy vessels, and the process can be painful.

"If you don't have discipline you wont have a successful program."
—Bear Bryant

DOMINANCE

"And God blessed them, and God said unto them, be fruitful, and multiply, and replenish the earth, and subdue it: and have dominion over the fish of the sea, and over the fowl of the air, and over every living thing that moves upon the earth." Genesis 1:28

Tennessee fans endured more than a decade of dominance by coach Paul "Bear" Bryant's fabled Alabama teams. It ranks as the most frustrating stretch of futility in the annals of UT football. And on Oct. 16, 1982, against the backdrop of a World's Fair, it came to an end. The World's Fair, in the '82 season, virtually brushed against the stadium gates, with Midway rides and booths extending along the river below the south end zone. The then second-largest crowd in Neyland Stadium history, 95,342, showed up to see the Vols face the No. 2-ranked Crimson Tide. The Vols were a 13-point underdog, and why not? After posing at the World's Fair site for the 1982 media brochure cover, they promptly got upset by Duke in the season opener. They were a modest 2-2-1 while Alabama came to Knoxville 5-0, fresh off a win over third-ranked Penn State. Indeed, it was a transitional afternoon. Bryant would retire at the end of the season, and three months after the Vols' victory he was dead. Tennessee racked up three more consecutive wins over Alabama. The Big Orange party lived on long after the World's Fair closed down.

The overwhelming majority of Christians do not take seriously the mandate we have as stewards over the creation. Christians generally relegate their faith to the "private" (internal) sphere, ignoring the world around them, or, when they are involved in the public sphere (economics, agriculture, charity, etc.) they simply follow the orders of the "principalities and powers" of the dominant culture.

There is no neutrality. Every human action must be done to the glory of God, in accord with His Word [sidebar]. This means Christians must consider the implications of the Dominion Mandate, and reclaim every area of life, every aspect of human culture, all human action—even "politics"—and place them under the Lordship of Christ.

"I borrowed, or stole more football coaching philosophy from Bob Neyland than anybody."

—Bear Bryant

EDUCATION

o o o o o o o o o o o o o o o o o o o o o o o o o o o o o o
"For with much wisdom comes much sorrow; the more education, the more grief." Ecclesiastes 1:18

Bear Bryant was introduced at an alumni banquet in Dothan shortly after he returned to Alabama. In the introduction it was told of his football accomplishments and was mentioned that he had "attended" the University of Alabama. Later on Bear told the person who introduced him, "Next time you introduce me, make sure you say I graduated from the University." He was proud of that degree, although he didn't get it until he was an assistant coach a year or so after he finished playing football.

In our pursuit of status and wealth, we have made education an idol. We have worshiped it, and we have used it to try to fill the void in ourselves, which can only be filled with God. And where has all this education gotten us? It's left us empty and unfulfilled, living lives without purpose or meaning. It's also left many of us deeply in debt. And we have begun to covet each other's levels of learning. We've become a society that feels it needs to "keep up with the Joneses" as far as degrees are concerned.

The Bible gives some clear warnings about placing too much value on education. Besides the verses above written by Solomon, Paul writes that "Knowledge puffs up, but love builds up." Too much education has a tendency to make us arrogant and prideful, and it can hinder our relationships with others and with God. Paul says: "Stop fooling yourselves. If you think you are wise by this world's standards, you will have to become a fool so you can become wise by God's standards. For the

wisdom of this world is foolishness to God." Paul was a highly educated man, yet he warns us here that striving to gain worldly wisdom
can hinder us from accepting the wisdom from above which can save
us. That's one of the reasons why Jesus said, "I tell you the truth, anyone who will not receive the kingdom of God like a little child will
never enter it." Children have a tendency to be humble and dependent,
while highly educated people often demonstrate more arrogant and
self-reliant attitudes. So what are Christians to do about their education? It's simple. Seek God. Then you'll get only the amount of education you really need, and He will provide the finances and the grace
you need to excel in your schoolwork. He'll even open doors of opportunity when the time comes.

"Learn from others. Ask questions. Be a good listener.

—Bear Bryant

END OF AN ERA

o o o o o o o o o o o o o o o o o o o o o o o o o o o o o o o o
"Now brothers about times and dates we do not need to write
to you. For you know very well that the day of the Lord will
come like a thief in the night. While people are saying peace
and safety destruction will come upon them suddenly, as
labor pains on a pregnant woman and they will not escape."
1 Thessalonians 5:1-3

On December 29, 1982, sports history was made and an era ended
with Bryant's final game, the <u>Liberty Bowl.</u> It was the same bowl he
had taken the Tide to in his first year as head coach. In a last rally of
respect for the man who had brought the Tide from mediocre to
mighty, the boys defeated Illinois twenty-one to fifteen. With three
hundred twenty-three career wins, Bryant was lauded as the winningest
coach in college football history.

Jesus said, "My kingdom is not of this world," and until the era or
"world to come" does come, Christ's kingdom will not control the
earth. And for this we are taught to hope and pray.

The other finale is also the end of an era, and, although it involves a
relocation it is truly a finale. This finale, however, has far reaching consequences for all those involved. The finale, the Great White Throne
Judgement of God. At this finale there will be no joy, no festive mood.
There will, however, be weeping as those involved realize an opportunity lost, and sigh's of sorrow as those involved stand before God to be
judged, having on some previous occasion spurned the offer of salvation from this judgment. God is also merciful in that because man is
unable to save himself from the penalty of sin, the Father sent His only

begotten Son, Jesus Christ, into the world, and He gave His life at Calvary that by His Blood He might pay the penalty for all those who trust in Him alone to save them. Let Jesus do that which you cannot, save you from the judgment to come, and enter your name into the Lamb's Book of Life. A simple prayer, "Jesus, please save me from the judgment to come. Amen" and your name will be entered into the book.

> *'I am the one who will decide when my career is over. They wont have to ask me to quit the way they did Adolph Rupp. I will know the time. As long as I am getting those chills up my back, as long as I know I am contributing toward another national championship, I will be around. And the only way you can measure that is by winning. There is no other way.'*

> —Bear Bryant

FABLE

II Timothy 4:4 "…and they shall turn away their ears from the truth, and shall be turned unto fables."

The fabled Bama coach concluded his Tide career with a 232-46-9 record (.824 win %). His 1961, 1964, 1965, 1973, 1978, and 1979 teams all won National Championships. In 1981, he broke Amos Alonzo Stagg's record of 314 coaching victories and finished a combined career record of 323-85-17. Under Bryant, Alabama had 25 winning seasons and was selected for bowl games 24 times. He was named national coach of the year 3 times, SEC coach of the year 10 times and was inducted into the National Football Foundation College Football Hall of Fame in 1986.

Over the past few decades, new Bible translations have been popping up like popcorn. Many strong Christians have stood their ground and continued to believe, read, and study only the Authorized King James Bible. Many others, however, have forsaken the Book that God has used for centuries. Such people have fallen for smooth advertising schemes and have actually started believing that the modern versions are superior to the King James Bible. It's very sad that most Christians today have not taken time to study the subject thoroughly enough to see what is really happening.

FABLE: New Translations are needed to bring the archaic Old English language up to date. People have trouble understanding the language of the King James Bible.

FACT: The King James language is NOT hard to understand. Most of the so-called "archaic" words are explained by the context of the passage or by comparing the passage with other passages in the Bible where the same word is used. Heady and high-minded people resent the King James language because it is plain and simple, and it isn't in tune with their high-minded vocabulary. In fact, the Grade Level Indicator of the Flesch-Kincaid research company says the King James language is EASIER to understand than the new versions.

I certainly agree that the language of the King James Bible is a unique language, but why shouldn't it be? It's the WORD OF GOD!

"If all the stories they tell about me benefits the University of Alabama, then it doesn't bother me."

—Bear Bryant

FALSE WITNESS

○ ○
"Do not bear false witness against your neighbor." Exodus
20:16

Joe Namath threw three touchdown passes in his first game, a 35-0 lashing of Georgia, but the game would become more famous as the subject of a 1963 Saturday Evening Post article charging Bryant and Georgia AD Wally Butts had conspired to "fix" the game.

The accusation infuriated Bryant and both men successfully sued the Post. In fact, it wasn't the first time the Post had targeted Bryant. He had earlier sued over an article that charged him with brutal coaching methods.

Have you heard any wild stories lately? Or, have you shared a story you possibly heard from someone else factual or a little slanted? I have heard a few stories, and I use the term stories loosely, from some fellow brothers and sisters in Christ. As you recall the commandment teaches us about false testimony.

If you are confronted with a story that is unfavorable about another brother or sister, or makes you feel uncomfortable as a Christian, please confront the messenger, and also bring the message to the attention of the one who is being slandered or betrayed.

While driving home a few weeks ago, I heard a speaker on the radio tell his listeners to take a challenge of trying to go for two weeks without passing on a rumor, AND if one comes your way, step out of your comfort zone and put the rumor to rest. Are you up for a challenge? Please ask the Holy Spirit to give you and our congregation the strength to remain steadfast through 14 days as we struggle with keeping the 8th commandment.

> *"I dreaded a the trial because I feared that the Post would bring in some sensational witness who would testify to some lie, that I'd done this, that and other."*

—Bear Bryant

FEAR OF FAILURE

○ ○
"Men's hearts fail them for fear and for looking after those
things which are coming on earth; for the powers of heaven
shall be shaken." Luke 21:26

Fear of failing Bear Bryant was important in the formula for success at
the collegiate level. Bear perfected the perfect combination for success.
He did that by pushing his players to the limit, to a level they didn't
know existed. But after pushing his players until they dropped, he
would go over and put an arm around their shoulder and say," I just
want you to be the best you can be. I know what is inside you. I know
what you are capable of doing on the football field." When a player got
a compliment like that from Coach Bryant, or just a pat on the back,
they just wanted to melt on the spot. Moments like that would over-
whelm a player and make them more determined to play that much
harder for him.

If we fear anything other than God, we are deceived. God is the only
thing in the universe worthy of fear. Satan, of course, would disagree
and has made an industry out generating bogus fear. His weapons are
horror movies, anxieties, worries, nightmares, phobias, panic attacks,
demons, etc. Satan wants the fear due God. To be sure, Satan is truly a
terrifying master to those under his care, but those "in Christ" have
been purchased from his mastery and need not fear him any longer.
Whenever it is in our power, we should cut off any access Satan has to
our minds or hearts to plant bogus fear.

"Coach Bryant definitely motivated players to be at their best. A strange form of fear was an interesting part of that. He was a intimidating man, size wise, and was extremely demanding."

—Lee Roy Jordan

FIGHTING

o o o o o o o o o o o o o o o o o o o o o o o o o o o o o
"The Lord will fight for you, and you shall hold your peace
and remain at rest." Exodus 14:14

If Bear had lost more fights than he won one would suppose he would have gotten over the scrapping business earlier in his young life. One guy did whip him pretty good at a dance in Hot Springs. After the game at Warren, Bear got into a fight with a big red headed guy and he gave Bear the worst licking he ever took as a man or a boy. Another time he knocked out a guy who stayed unconscious for three days. Every hour Bear was awake he promised the Lord if he let him out the mess he had gotten himself into, he'd never have another fight. And Bear never had another one because he claimed to be a coward at heart anyway.

I once heard someone say that Christians lose more battles because they don't let God do their fighting for them. I believe that's true. There are many verses in the Bible that indicate that God is willing and able to do battle for us. Whether our battles are big or small, we should commit them to the Lord and ask Him to fight for us and show us what our part might be. It's important in times like these that we resist becoming fearful or anxious, because fear can cause us to react rashly, and to make poor decisions and costly mistakes. Fear can also make it more difficult for us to receive direction from the Lord. It's wiser for us to pray and stand on God's promises of victory, including Deuteronomy 28:13, which says, "You shall always have the upper hand." Most of all, we should remember that we are never to count on others to execute justice for us apart from God. For as Proverbs 29:26 NIV says,

59

"Many seek an audience with a ruler, but it is from the Lord that man gets justice." Everyone experiences conflict. Sometimes we cause it, and sometimes we're just caught in the middle of it. But no matter where conflict comes from, we are supposed to be people who make peace. That's what Jesus means. He's talking about people who can walk right into conflict—whether they asked for it or not—and turn it into peace. Ultimately, peace between people only comes when people have peace with God. Alone, people can make temporary peace. But only God can make peace permanent. That's part of what Jesus meant by "peacemakers." We are called not only to make peace with other people, but between people and God.

> *"Every man I had left on the team after the trip to Junction felt he could whip. Joe Louis on Saturday."*
>
> —Bear Bryant

FINISHING WHAT YOU START

○ ○
"I have fought the good fight, I have finished the race, and I
have kept the faith." 2 Timothy 4:7

Bryant was enamored of the University of Alabama. He had heard
about the Crimson Tide and Wallace Wade who had taken his men to
three Rose Bowls. While being recruited, the Arkansas head coach took
Bryant to Dallas to a college all-star game, but at the half Bryant
slipped out and listened to Alabama beat Washington State 24-0 in the
1931 Rose Bowl.

One day, University of Alabama assistant coach Hank Crisp came
to town to recruit Fordyce's talented Jordan twins. Crisp didn't sign
the twins but he was impressed enough with Bryant and offered him a
scholarship to Alabama. The only problem was Bryant was one class
short from graduating. It didn't matter. Bear jumped at the chance to
play for the Crimson Tide and moved to campus in 1931. He attended
and graduated from Tuscaloosa High while practicing with the Alabama team. He enrolled at Alabama soon after.

I read a humorous story about a bloodhound. He started chasing a
deer but a fox crossed his path, so he started chasing the fox instead.
After a while, a rabbit crossed his path, so the hound chased the rabbit.
Yet later, a mouse crossed his path and the hound chased the mouse
into a hole. The hound, which had begun his hunt on the trail of a
magnificent deer, ended up watching a mouse hole!

Most of us will laugh at the bloodhound. But if we stop and think, we'll realize that often we too are easily distracted. At times we may even be sidetracked from following Christ. It is so easy to start well but then run after things that cross our paths.

We need to take to heart the words of the apostle Paul. He told Timothy to focus on the purpose of his life and ministry

> *"Have a goal. And to reach that goal, you'd better have a plan. Have a plan that you believe in so strongly you'll never compromise."*
>
> —Bear Bryant

FIRM FOUNDATION

○ ○
"For no one can lay any foundation other than the one already laid, which is Jesus Christ." 1 Corinthians 3:11

While his first Texas A&M team had heart, guts, and determination, they finished the season 1-9, Bear's only losing record as a head coach. But the foundation had been layed and in 1956, the Aggies won the Southwest Conference championship. In 1957, halfback John David Crow won the Heisman Trophy, the only player coached by Bryant to receive the honor.

At this point in your life are you standing, spiritually speaking, on a firm foundation? Every person lives out his life, however consistently or inconsistently, on the basis of some foundational beliefs, upon some set of presuppositions that he considers to be true. These beliefs may be well thought out or they may be more or less held without ever having given them serious thought. Whatever your current beliefs are, you need to take the time to give them serious thought because there may be more at stake in your beliefs than you realize.

In saying that, Jesus clearly set forth the standard of God: perfection. For a person to be acceptable to God, his life, his thoughts, and his conduct must be perfect continually. If you are trusting in your "goodness" to get you to heaven, there is absolutely no room for error; you must be perfect. However, the Bible teaches that this is completely impossible.

"The ones that make it back to College Station will be the foundation we will build a winner on."

—Bear Bryant

GOALS

o o o o o o o o o o o o o o o o o o o o o o o o o o o o o o o o
"I press toward the goal for the prize of the high calling of
God in Jesus Christ." Philippians 3:14

Bear Bryant made a habit out of telling each freshman class that if they did everything he would guarantee them they would win a national championship before the graduated. He recruited 22 freshmen classes which he coached through their senior seasons More than one in four (six) won national titles' another one (1966,11-0, and the only unbeaten untied team in the country) should have won it and three others lost out on the championship by losing bowl games. With a lucky bounce here and there, Alabama could easily have won an outstanding 10 national championships in 25 years under Bear.

When you are playing golf, it is very important that you can see the flag, which marks the location of the hole. It's hard to tell where the hole is located without a flag marking the hole location. It is important to have a target to aim for. Golf teachers tell us that one of the important things to do when preparing to hit the ball is to line up with your target. It makes sense that if you don't take the target into consideration, you are very unlikely to ever hit it. Targets and goals play a very important part in our lives. For one thing, goals enable us to measure our progress, as we get closer to the goal. No matter how far you are from the hole, you can measure your progress with each stroke. Without a goal, you don't know whether you are making progress or not.

Goals also give you something to celebrate when you arrive. Without a goal, I'd have nothing to celebrate after either a good or a bad hole. A target also gives you a direction in which you are heading. Having a clear sense of direction is very helpful as I take one pitiful shot after another. In life, as in golf, it helps to have a goal or target toward which one is moving, to enable you to measure your progress, to give you something to celebrate, and to give you a sense of direction. Many people seem to go through life with no goals or with goals, which aren't worthy of their dedication and energy. I suggest that you choose a goal, which is worth pursuing. God's will and the Kingdom of God provide goals worthy of your attention. For instruction as to how to move toward these goals consult the Bible.

"Set goals—high goals—for you and your organization. When your organization has a goal to shoot for, you create teamwork, people working for a common good."

—Bear Bryant

GOD'S TIME

o o o o o o o o o o o o o o o o o o o o o o o o o o o o o o o o

'But do not forget this one thing, dear friends: With the Lord a day is like a thousand years, and a thousand years are like a day. The Lord is not slow in keeping his promise, as some understand slowness. He is patient with you, not wanting anyone to perish, but everyone to come to repentance.' 2 Peter 3:8-9

Alabama would field good teams through the ten years of the 60's, going 90-16-4. A 6-5 season in 1969 was the only disappointment but Bryant had successfully revitalized his alma mater, winning three national championships. Alabama was named Team of the Decade and Bryant the Coach of the Decade by an NCAA poll.

The Apostle Peter's readers should not lose heart because God seems slow at fulfilling His promises because He is patient, and also because He is not bound by time as we are.

The text says 'one day is like a thousand years'—the word 'like' shows that it is a figure of speech, called a simile, to teach that God is outside of time (because He is the Creator of time itself). In fact, the figure of speech is so effective in its intended aim precisely because the day is literal and contrasts so vividly with 1000 years—to the eternal Creator of time, a short period of time and a long period of time may as well be the same.

The fact that the passage is actually contrasting a short and long period can be shown by the fact that Peter is quoting Psalm 90:4 (Peter's statement 'do not forget' implies that his readers were expected to recall something, and this passage has this very teaching).

God's time is not our time.

"We didn't lose we just ran out of time."

—Bear Bryant

GOING FULL SPEED

o o o o o o o o o o o o o o o o o o o o o o o o o o o o o o o
Wherefore seeing we also are compassed about with so great
a cloud of witnesses, let us lay aside every weight, and the sin
which doth so easily beset us, and let us run with patience the
race that is set before us, Looking unto Jesus the author and
finisher of our faith; who for the joy that was set before him
endured the cross, despising the shame, and is set down at the
right hand of God.—Hebrews 12:1,2

Bear played offensive end and defensive tackle. Paul loved the game
and the challenges it presented. He was big and strong, but more
importantly he had a spirit and intensity rarely displayed by a high
school player. He played full-speed every second he was on the field.
Paul knew playing football for the Fordyce Redbugs would be his
ticket out.

Running is a fun sport. It is good exercise and helps me stay in
shape. There are some important things to know if you are going to
run a marathon. A marathon is a very long race of 10 kilometers [or use
miles equivalent] or more. You have to pace yourself. You just can't
run at full speed or you will give out before you can finish the race.
Another thing is that you can't take along much or it will slow you
down.

That is what it means to run God's race. We have to look to the
example our Lord Jesus gave us. We can't just do it on our own. If we
hold on to our old ways and habits of being a bad person (sin), then we
will not be able to finish the race. It will slow us down. If we rely on the

Lord Jesus, he will forgive us and we can put aside our sin. Then we can run at a steady pace, living a godly life. Just as a runner keeps his mind on the finish line, we can keep our eyes on Jesus as we go through our life here on earth.

Well, I have to be going now. Next time you put on a pair of running shoes, stop and ask yourself: Am I running my own race, or am I running God's race?

"You have to be willing to out-condition your opponents."

—Bear Bryant

GOOD INTENTIONS

"For the word of God is living, and active, and sharper than any two-edged sword, and piercing even to the dividing of soul and spirit, of both joints and marrow, and is able to discern the thoughts and intentions of the heart." Hebrews 4:12

The lives Bear Bryant touched were the most telling witness to his greatness. Bryant understood that there was more to a player than a strong arm or fast legs. The building of character was essential to the building of a winning team. "Intentions over the years were to help the players to be better persons every day, to help themselves, to teach a lesson on and off the field," he said.

I remember a recent story in the news concerning a man who was at a neighbor's party. He returned home to get something that was needed at the party and heard a noise, which he thought, was a burglar. He tracked down the burglar who was hiding in a closet, opened the door, and shot the intruder to death. Immediately the man realized that he had shot and killed his daughter. Later the man learned that his daughter had been hiding in the closet as part of a game or joke. I would like for us to think about factors that determine whether good intentions have a good or bad ending. We can learn our first lesson from this story. The man began with good intentions—to protect his property from an intruder. But, the result was tragic because of the choices he made in accomplishing his intent.

We may have good intentions, but Jesus teaches us to count the cost before acting to accomplish our intent. I am sure you can relate to this lesson. Who has not seen good intentions spoiled because of poor decisions? Good intentions, in and of themselves, are good. But the choices we make in accomplishing our intent renders the end result good or bad. Good intentions begin with a thought and end with an action. Before acting, always count the cost—or you may be sorry. If you do not believe me, just ask the man who shot his daughter.

> *"I was a little too hard on my early teams, I thought that was what they needed."*
>
> —Bear Bryant

GOOD NAME

"Choose a good name over great riches, for being held in high
esteem is better than having silver or gold." Proverbs 22:1

When the Paul W. Bryant Museum opened recently in Tuscaloosa,
Alabama, more than 100 of his namesakes were on hand for the big
occasion. "When you name your kid after someone, it says a lot about
what you want that child to be like," said Ken Gaddy, head of the
museum. "I think these people liked the attitude, the work ethic, the
respect for others that coach Bryant had." Among those attending were
12-year-old Chad Bryant Gilbert, 27-year-old Paul Bryant Henderson
and 28-year-old Matthew Bryant Gilmer. According to the Interactive
Sports Wire, young Chad Bryant Gilbert's mother learned she was
pregnant with Chad the night "The Bear" died of a heart attack in
Tuscaloosa. Paul Bryant Henderson said, "One of the first stories my
parents told me was that when I was a baby, coach Bryant held me in
the parking lot at Legion Field while he signed an autograph for my
dad. I cried for about a week when he died." Matthew Bryant Gilmer's
father, Creed Gilmer, was an all-Southeastern Conference defensive
end who played for Bryant. "Coach Bryant would frequently scream
'Gilmer!' he said. "One day my father vowed to name the child after
him so he could scream, 'Bryant!' " Ask yourself: "If I did not have a
name, how could I identify myself? If I had no name, who would I be?"

Your name is extremely important. Your name is your life! It is how
you identify yourself. It is how others identify you. The more insight
you have into the powerful influence of your name, the greater opportunity to enjoy the success you are capable of achieving.

'Paul' This popular name was that of Apostle Paul to the Gentiles, six popes, and more than thirty five saints. It is Latin in origin and it means 'small'.

'William' This popular Christian name has many variations in different European languages. There are more than forty saints of this name. It originates from German and means 'strenuous guardian'.

"I don't know what kind of name Bryant is, where the family got started, but Daddy's people were from Georgia and were farmers."

—Bear Bryant

GOOD TIMING

○ ○
"But when the right time finally came, God sent his own
Son. He came as the son of a human mother and lived under
Jewish law." Galatians 4:4

After the 1941 season, he was invited to be interviewed for the head coaching job at Arkansas. Sure enough, the job was his. He was only 28 years old. Bryant was driving back home, and he was proud. But the day was December 7, 1941, and he overheard on the car radio that the Japanese had bombed Pearl Harbor. Someone else would have to be head coach at Arkansas. The very next day, coach Bryant became lieutenant commander Bryant in the U.S. Navy. He was stationed on the USS Uruguay in North Africa. While Bryant saw no actual fighting, he did escape death when his ship was rammed in February 1943. Many of his shipmates drowned, but Bryant luckily survived.

I've heard it said that we are the microwave generation. When we want something, we want it now! I believe it is true that people are losing the skill of waiting patiently. It isn't easy to wait. We can picture in our minds what we want and we want it to become reality as quickly as possible. When we have a problem we think we have to do something about it right away. We don't want to have to wait. We know that God's timing is perfect, but we can't see His timing. We can only see our point of view. Sometimes we think God didn't hear us. He hears us. He won't be one minute late with the response. His timing is perfect.

"Success in anything is a matter of timing, no matter what you do."

—Bear Bryant

GREATNESS

"Truly, I say to you, among those born of women there has not arisen anyone greater than John the Baptist." Matthew 11:11

The 1979 Alabama team (12-0) was one of the best of Paul Bryant's teams—which is really saying something, considering "The Bear" won six national championships in his quarter century at Alabama. The '79 Tide rolled to a 12-0 record behind a balanced attack that closed out its national championship season with a 24-9 victory over Arkansas in the Sugar Bowl in front of a record crowd of 77,468.

The Tide shutout five of its opponents during the season and never allowed an opponent to score more than 18 points. The secondary was key to the Tide's success, with Tommy Wilcox and Jim Bob Harris the mainstays.

How do you measure greatness? The world measures greatness a number of ways. For example, athletic achievement, political power or position, business success, academic degrees, and the list goes on. Have you ever stopped to think about what God considers to be great or His thoughts concerning greatness?

"What did John the Baptist do that would cause Jesus to say John the Baptist was the greatest"? The purpose of John the Baptist was to prepare the hearts and minds of those living during his time to receive and accept the coming Messiah. That's It! He was not a man of wealth, education, athleticisms, business, or politics. His job was to prepare people, to accept Christ.

I encourage you today; if you want to be great in the eyes of God, do what John the Baptist did. In every area of our life we need to do exactly what John the Baptist did, that is preparing the hearts around us to receive and accept the coming KING, Jesus Christ. Paul reminds us that some plant and some water, but the Lord makes all things grow. If you want to do something great for God, I challenge you to begin to cultivate the hearts and minds of those around you....

"A great performer can give a great performance and lose. A great player will do the things it takes to win"

—Bear Bryant

GRIEF

o o o o o o o o o o o o o o o o o o o o o o o o o o o o o o o
"Surely he hath borne our griefs, and carried our sorrows; yet
we did esteem him stricken, smitten of God, and afflicted."
Isaiah 53:4

I remember the moment Coach Paul "Bear" Bryant announced he was
retiring…that he even spoke softly that he did not know how long he
would live after he left coaching, but he made plans to do a lot of
things before that time…Unfortunately that moment arrived, January
26th, 1983. Alabama grieved for one like no other…and I too remember standing with hundreds of others along the way as Coach Paul
"Bear" Bryant took his final ride out of Tuscaloosa to Birmingham to
his resting place. Anyone who lived in Tuscaloosa during his era will
always remember him. I know I will…

Does it sound strange to imagine God grieving? In the Bible, we
read of several instances in which people or events moved God to grief
on Earth. In Genesis, God grieves at the loss of a close relationship
with humans (Genesis 6:6). God can be moved to grief when we turn
away from his will for our lives (Ephesians 4:30). What is the grief of
God like? Is it a process like our own, filled with feelings of sadness and
loss?

We don't know. But the choice of words in these Bible passages
seems to tell us that, in our loss, we have a Friend who has been where
we stand—who knows exactly what it's like to feel that loss, pain, and
disappointment. He shares our tears and our sadness, and He is there
as we struggle to emerge whole again from this experience of broken-
ness. And He promises us that our grief and pain won't last forever:

"I remember passing by a little house, there was a man on his front porch. When the processional passed, he stopped what he was doing. There were tears running down his face. I doubt he had ever seen Coach Bryant, or met him, but he was crying for a man so many loved. That was a sad time for a lot of people, an uncountable number, thousands upon thousands who loved Coach Bryant."

—Linda Knowles, secretary

GUT CHECK

"The refining pot is for silver, and the furnace for gold, But the Lord tests the hearts." Proverbs 17:3

It was really unbelievable how the victory over Penn St. in the 1979 Sugar bowl shaped up. But it's exactly the type of game Bear Bryant always talked about, winning with defense in the fourth quarter when the chips are down and a national championship at stake. It was funny how during the pregame practice the day before that Murray Legg, a senior safety, said off the cuff," This is where the game is going to be won or lost." Alabama was working on their goal line defense on the same end of the Superdome that they stopped Penn St. Then it was Murray who said,' This is a gut check" as Penn St. got ready to make those runs on third down and fourth down. That made Murray famous, because Alabama fans refer to that as The Gut Check. But Murray wasn't the first person to say that. Coach Bryant used to talk about gut checks all the time at practice.

Gut checks build endurance. We do not like it. Perhaps we even detest the gut checks of our souls and lives. However, with courage, with wisdom, with understanding, and with patience we can indeed count our trials as blessings. With wisdom, we can count our trials as a great joy. In the middle of the gut check when we become weary and want to walk away from our trials, the Lord calls out to us to finish the work rather than quit. Mature people are complete people. If mature people lack something then they are wise enough to either overcome or compensate for what they lack or they pass the gut check by building upon their disadvantage in a constructive way. Gut checks, trials, or suffering can be taken advantage of. Perseverance becomes self-reinforcing because we learn from it. God does not inflict the suffering or wound, however, God assigns a purpose, goal, and meaning to the suffering after Satan inflicts the wound. The next time you don't "feel" like a Christian, do a gut check. Go to God and ask, "Have I sinned against you?"

"There is no substitute for guts."

—Bear Bryant

HADES

o o o o o o o o o o o o o o o o o o o o o o o o o o o o o o o
"Ye serpents, ye generation of vipers, how can ye escape the
damnation of hell?" Matthew 23:33

Bryant knew he had to instill discipline and toughness in order for
A&M to compete. One day during summer practice, he loaded the
unsuspecting Aggies in two buses and headed west to Junction, Texas
for what was arguably the toughest training camp in football history.
Bryant started with 48 players but only came back with 29. Gene Stallings, who was one of Bryant's players at the time, was quoted as saying,
"We left in two buses and came back in one, and that one was half
full." Bryant put his team through hell at Junction because he wanted
to build character and have his players realize that things were going to
be done his way.

Of all biblical concepts, hell is one of the most mysterious and
feared. The word "hell" appears 54 times in the Bible, 30 times in the
Old Testament, 24in the New Testament. It is represented by the
church to mean a place of eternal fiery torture for those who don't
believe in the Christ as Savior, and in extreme cases those who question
the authority of the church. This obviously means that the majority of
humanity is destined for eternal fiery torture.

What does the Bible really teach? Is it the Creator's intention to
punish everlastingly those who, during their few short years of life on
earth, fail to measure up to His standards of faith and obedience? Can
a loving God, who sent His Son to be man's redeemer, be also a merci-
less autocrat who takes revenge on men, women, and children who
never had a real opportunity to know Him and accept of His grace?

One of the classic problems that people bring up is: How can a God of love send anybody to Hell? Well, there are several answers to that. One of course is that God doesn't send anyone to Hell. You send yourself there. God has done everything He possibly can to keep you out of Hell and still leave you as a person with free will and not just a robot. That's the way He made us—after His image, after His likeness, the power to say "yes" or the power to say "no," the power to reject our own Creator, and of course to take the consequences.

> *"Over the years I have thought about Junction, I haven't been sure I did the right thing."*
>
> —Bear Bryant

HEAD MAN

"For the husband is the head of the wife, even as Christ is the head of church: and He is the savior of the body." Ephesians 5:23

After serving four years in the Navy, it was time for Bear to get back to work and to forge a career in the sport he so dearly loved. He became head coach at the North Carolina Pre-Flight School where he coached All-American QB Otto Graham. George Marshall, owner of the Washington Redskins, offered Bryant an assistant's job, but Bryant wanted to be a head coach. Marshall called Curly Byrd, president of Maryland and recommended Bryant for their vacant head coaching job. Byrd soon offered him the Terps job and at age 32, Bryant was finally a head coach.

Every family should have someone to direct them. God has assigned to the husband the responsibility of being the head of the wife and the family.

The husband should not treat his wife with rudeness or harshness. The Bible says she is like a fragile vessel (1 Peter 3:7). With this the apostle Peter wanted to say that the woman should be treated delicately, because she is physically more weak that the man. The man should love his wife with the same intensity that he loves himself.

In ancient Greece there was a philosopher name Diogenes who was walking through the city carrying a lantern. One day someone asked him what he was doing with that lighted lantern. His answer was that he was looking for someone a husband with qualities, which make him worthy to hold the title of a husband.

"A head coach is stupid if he doesn't do what is best for his people."

—Bear Bryant

HIDDEN TALENT

o o o o o o o o o o o o o o o o o o o o o o o o o o o o o o o
"Again the kingdom of heaven is like hidden treasure in a
field; the which when a man has found it, he hides, and for
joy there of goes and sells all that he has, and buys that field."
Mathew 13:44

In the early seventies, Alabama's backfield coach found a prospective
quarterback that he was sure could be the key to a future championship
team. He prepared his report and put together a film of the prospect in
action. Coach Bryant, along with all his assistant coaches were shown
the film.

Halfway though the running of the film, Coach Bryant stood,
walked to the screen and pointed at the left tackle, "Who's that?" he
asked. None of the assistants knew the player's name. He instructed
them to find out, and then added, "It's OK to go for the quarterback
but get the left tackle."

Jim Bunch was the left tackle in question. Not a single college, not
even those in his home state of West Virginia, was recruiting him.
Every major college in the country was recruiting his teammate, the
quarterback.

Alabama didn't get the quarterback from West Virginia. They
recruited a kid from Beaver Falls, PA, named Joe Namath, to be their
quarterback.

However, just as Coach Bryant instructed, Alabama did successfully
recruit Jim Bunch. In his four-year college career, Jim started every
game. He was named All-American two of those years and during Jim

Bunch's career, Alabama won three of Coach Bryant's six national championships.

Our talents and skills will multiply the more that we use them for His sake. The more we work at developing the gifts of the Lord the more our abilities seem to expand. When we die we will be asked of the Lord what we did with the talents that He gave us. If we forget that all things come from God and even this special talents need to be given back to the Lord in service to Him for his glory and purpose. The man who didn't increase the use of his talents didn't really share any interest in helping his master be successful.

"Find the talent and relate to it."

—Bear Bryant

HOMEWORK

"I have glorified You on the earth by completing the work
You gave Me to do." John 17:4

Bear Bryant always did his homework and he apparently made up his
mind to hire Hayden Riley as a recruiter before he ever talked to him.
Bear said he had been recommended as knowing more people in Alabama and the Southeast than anyone. Riley was given only a one-year
contract until he signed Lee Roy Jordan.

One secret to successful teaching: good assignment sheets. Every
time I assign homework, I give out a sheet with all of the instructions
(deadline, length). I've learned the hard way that if I try to read off the
assignment details and expect students to remember them, I'm asking
for trouble. With an assignment sheet, students know exactly what I
am expecting. If they have questions, they can refer to the sheet. I don't
have to worry about forgetting to tell them important details. The
expectations are there, written down. Paul had an assignment for Timothy, his young disciple. No, it wasn't a research paper. In 1 Timothy
6:11-16, Paul laid out his expectations for him, listing the challenges
he would face as a young pastor. The assignment is so simple it's intimidating: flee the love of money and pursue righteousness, godliness,
faith, love, endurance, and gentleness. As the list demonstrates, the
goals of the Christian life are not tasks, but character qualities. Too
often, when we think about pleasing God, our list is a bunch of accomplishments. God is looking for us to develop Christ like virtues; the rest
happens naturally after that. So what is your assignment? Get your
hands on a Bible dictionary and look up each of the qualities Paul

named. Identify one that you need to work on. Then, as verse 12 says, "fight the good fight of the faith." Of course, we can play hide-and-seek with school assignments, and my students do…RARELY. But when we consider that this assignment is made in the sight of God and Jesus Christ, it becomes a lot more serious! You have your assignment. The deadline is tricky. On the one hand, you will work on it every day of your life. On the other hand, it is due every day. Your challenge is to display those qualities more and more. So when your friends ask if you have any homework, smile—and not because of that history paper. Recognize instead how much God must believe in you to give you such a tough assignment, and to fully trust that in the power of His Holy Spirit you will ace it

"Work hard. There is no substitute for hard work."

—Bear Bryant

HOUNDSTOOTH HAT

○ ○
"Every man praying or prophesying, having his head covered, dishonors his head," 1 Corinthians 11:4

The Bear Bryant museum averages 40,000 visitors a year and features a larger-than-life bronze bust of the Bear and a re-creation of his office, complete with houndstooth hat and coat on the rack, as if he had just stepped out. There are relics of the glory days: license plates that read ala'bear'ma 1981 and full bottles of Coca-Cola bearing his likeness and a year-by-year listing of the Crimson Tide's records during his 25 seasons as coach. Most excessive is the Waterford crystal replica of his hat, which rotates slowly on a black velvet pillow, encased in glass and perched on a pedestal.

The head Paul refers to dishonoring is not the man's own head, but Christ, who has authority—or headship—over every Christian. In the previous verse, Paul said, "But I want you to know that the head of every man is Christ, the head of the woman is man, and the head of Christ is God." Paul's main point here is men shouldn't keep their hats on when addressing the Lord in worship. I presume from that, if you aren't praying or preaching, which is what prophesying means, it was fine with Paul to wear a hat in church. But please don't try that on my say-so. I've seen young men in church wearing ball caps and have resisted an almost overwhelming urge to remove it for them. The real issue here is recognizing that Christ has the authority over us, and just as no man would address a king while wearing his hat, neither should we address our King while our head is covered. With the men, the issue was a sign of respect for the authority of Christ. And with the women, the issue was the same, a cultural one.

"Mama always taught me not to wear a hat indoors."

—Bear Bryant, when asked why he didn't have his hat on during the Sugar Bowl played in the Superdome

INHERITANCE

"And now, brethren, I commend you to God, and to the
word of his grace, which is able to build you up, and to give
you an inheritance among all them which are sanctified."
Acts 20:32

In 1954, Bear packed up and headed west to Texas A&M. He had the
master formula for success, and wanted to test it out at another school.
But Bryant inherited an awful program with few good players. Texas
A&M was a tough place to lure players to. No girls, no glamour, military uniforms and, at first glance, the school looked more like a peni-
tentiary than a college campus.

We have a wonderful hope in the inheritance reserved for us in
heaven. When things go wrong here below, it is wonderful to think
that we have an inheritance of unimaginable glory and beauty, which
can never be spoiled. God has made us all his sons (regardless of
whether we are male or female). We are all equally heirs of God.

Inheritance includes God being present with us daily, supplying our
needs, and giving us comfort. Inheritance allows us to look forward to
being with God in Heaven for eternity. We must be willing to share
God's Good News with all people. Someday, God's patience will run
out, and He will stop sending invitations. Those who have rejected His
invitation or tried to make their own rules will not be allowed into
God's Kingdom.

"Texas A&M did not lack for football tradition. I inherited those doggone wonderful Aggie Exes."

—Bear Bryant

INSINUATIONS

"Let the proud be ashamed; for they treated me wrongfully with insinuations; but I will meditate in His bidding." Psalms 119:78

Insinuations were made about many things concerning Bear Bryant and his gambling was one of them. He never tried to hide that. He would be a fool if he did. He would tell anybody that wanted to know that he had cashed checks at racetracks and in Las Vegas and he played the stock market.

The insinuation was made that he bet on the 1962 Georgia Tech game, that 7-6 loss. The story suggested that he had thrown the game because Alabama had a first down on the Tech 14 with about a minute to play and instead of kicking a field goal; Alabama threw a pass that was intercepted.

Well, Alabama was a passing team that year and anybody with half a mind for football could look at the films and see that the receiver on the play was wide open. The ball hit his hands and bounced up in the air, and that is how Tech intercepted it. He makes the catch and Alabama is on the 3-yard line with plenty of time to score a touchdown and in surer position for a field goal. He misses and Alabama still has three downs.

Tech had a good defensive team and Alabama wasn't good at running the ball. Alabama had Joe Namath that year, and what runner could run better that Joe could pass?

The big mistake of the day was going for two points after their touchdown.

Insinuation, in the Scripture, means to make crooked. This means that they deceived him in their dealings with them. We remember who the proud are. They are too proud to humble themselves and receive the Lord. They are lost. This would be a common practice of someone who was lost. They would have no conscience, and they would do whatever it took to benefit them. He is saying, that even though they dealt with him in a crooked manner, he will not do the same to them, because he remembers the teachings of God's law. He is saying, I will do it your way, Lord.

"When I was a young coach I used to say,' Treat everybody alike.'
That's bull. Treat everybody fairly."

—Bear Bryant

LEADERSHIP

"Behold, I have given him for a witness to the people, a leader
and commander to the people." Isaiah 55:4

Bear Bryant had a special relationship with his quarterbacks and with a
purpose. He wanted them, as on the field leaders, to have the respect
and confidence of the other players. To accomplish that he spent extra
time with them and often shared meals with them, transferring his own
stature to them as he gave them extra lessons on the game of football.
The relationship that Bryant had with his quarterbacks was partly
responsible for his having five of them make All-America, nine all-conference and nine of them to play pro football.

If we were to ask how to define leadership in one single word, the
word would be influence. President Harry Truman often referred to
leaders as people who can get others to do what they don't want to
do—and make them like doing it. Leaders are generally the hardest
workers on a team. They are the first to come to practice and the last
ones to leave. During practice they lead by example, not by their
words. Leaders know the team's goals, and know what needs to be
accomplished. They realize that practice is the key to future victory.
Real leaders hate to lose more than they enjoy winning. They are
always willing to pay a price. Their work ethic and their attitude
becomes contagious. Leaders are individuals who know where they are
going, and that is generally where the team wants to go: to the victory
stand, the rest of the team will follow. Being a leader is a tough and
demanding job. Sometimes the pressure falls only on their shoulders.
When you invest much, then there is a lot at stake. Most team leaders

will tell you that the rewards are worth the risk. Any leader realizes that you can't do it alone—that is what team is all about. Perhaps God has put you in a place of leadership on your team. If He has, ask yourself at this very moment, where are you leading those who are following you?

"Leaders are self starters. They say, "Let's go" and lead. They don't say, "Sic' em" and step back to watch the fighters do the work."

—Bear Bryant

LEARNING FROM THE MASTER

o o o o o o o o o o o o o o o o o o o o o o o o o o o o o o

"Go and learn what that means, I will have mercy, and not
sacrifice; for I am not come to call the righteous, but sinners
to repentance." Matthew 9:13

Gene Stallings is best known for his outstanding coaching career.

His style—influenced by mentor Paul "Bear" Bryant. A coach who,
in just three seasons, returned Alabama football to the glory it had once
known, leading his team to the national championship in 1992. With
all eyes on the Tide that year, Stallings and his staff produced Alabama's first perfect season since 1979 by winning the Sugar Bowl and
finishing 13-0 for the season. That year, he was named as the SEC
Coach of the Year by numerous organizations. Born in Paris, Texas,
Stallings played football at Paris High School. He went on to play for
Bear Bryant at Texas A&M University in 1954. Remaining at Texas
A&M as a graduate assistant coach, he later moved to Alabama as a
full-time assistant coach under Bryant. He returned to Texas A&M in
1965, taking his first head coaching job at age 29. His Aggie team won
the Southwest Conference Championship in 1967 and defeated Bryant's Crimson Tide in the 1968 Cotton Bowl. Stallings spent the next
14 years with Tom Landry and the Dallas Cowboys, winning seven
division titles, three conference championships and a Super Bowl. He
made his NFL head-coaching debut in 1986 with the St. Louis Cardi-
nals. Returning to Alabama in 1990, he concluded his coaching career
there in 1996.

Jesus of Nazareth is one of the most attractive people of all time. But who is he really? In his lifetime, he gathered around him 12 disciples who walked with him—literally—for three years. Today his nominal followers number in the billions. But how many actually walk with him today?

Becoming a faithful disciple of Jesus is a process. Jesus took twelve men with him to walk with him day-by-day and live with him for three years. The training wasn't all at once, though some of their experiences stood out like mountaintops. But many of the lessons centered on the incidents of life, a healing, the observation of a tree, the reaction of Jesus' enemies. Little by little he shared with them how he looked at life. He helped them see what was important and what was not. It was a journey, a process, and it took time.

"You can learn as much from your players as you can teach them."

—Bear Bryant

LOSING GRACEFULLY

Because of his sharp dress and graceful demeanor, Bud Wilkinson possessed an air of dignity. But that didn't stop Bear Bryant from chiding his friend. Some critics believed that Wilkinson amassed his winning streaks against weaklings from the Big Seven. After Kentucky's victory in the 1951 Sugar Bowl, Bryant told Wilkinson, "I guess I just showed you that the big fellers of the SEC are a little tougher than the little fellers from that Big Seven Conference." Bryant then stood in awe as Wilkinson walked gracefully into the Kentucky dressing room and gave a brief speech, congratulating the winning team. At the time, Bryant was known as the most ungracious loser in college football. But from that day forward, he didn't mind repeating Wilkinson's gesture. Some say that Wilkinson's demeanor helped bring out the kinder, gentler side of Bryant.

It happens every season. Poor sports spoil games. Fans badmouth umpires. Hotheaded coaches throw temper tantrums. Players turn rivalries into slugfests. That's why the first basketball game of the 1989-90 season between two longtime rivals was so noteworthy. It was whisker close. With just 6 seconds to play, Hope College trailed Calvin by one point. Hope brought the ball down court. A shot was taken, and the ball went through the hoop. Hope fans erupted in jubilation, but so did Calvin fans, thinking the shot was made after the final buzzer. The officials ruled. The buzzer had sounded. The score: Calvin 77, Hope 76.

The president of Hope College recalls the fans' reactions: "They didn't scream in protest or tear up the seats. They turned to each other and said, 'What a great game! What a great rivalry!' " It was sportsmanship at its best. Students and parents from two Christian schools acted as Christians should act.

The game of life holds even greater disappointments. But Christians have God's wisdom, which James describes as "peaceable, gentle, willing to yield, full of mercy and good fruits, without partiality and without hypocrisy." When we let Christ control us, we can lose with grace because we are hoping in God. Close calls allow us the opportunity to be good sports-and real winners.

"If you lose with humility, then you can come back."

—Bear Bryant

MAMA

"Honor thy father and thy mother: that thy days may be long upon the land which the LORD thy God gives you." Exodus 20:12

The once proud Alabama football program had fallen on tough times, winning only 4 games in the previous three years. The decision was made to fire J. B. (Ears) Whitworth after suffering a 28-0 loss to TCU and a 40-0 blowout at the hands of Auburn. A Press Conference was held in the Shamrock Hotel in Houston, Texas, and Paul "Bear" Bryant was announced as the new head coach of the Alabama Crimson Tide. Approximately one month earlier Coach Bryant was in the same hotel meeting with officials about coming to Alabama. A major item that concerned Bryant was the feeling of his former coach and the then athletic director, Hank Crisp. After Coach Crisp assured him that he wanted him to return and the AD's job was his, the deal was sealed. Bryant called a meeting with his A&M players and simply stated, "Gentlemen, I've heard Mama calling," he told them, "and now I'm going home." The Alabama Crimson Tide Football program was about to enjoy an era that may never be matched again in the history of college football.

Motherhood is both a demanding and a rewarding profession. Unfortunately, the reward often comes much later in life, but a prime characteristic of the good mother is unselfishness; she can wait for the final realization of her rewards. No one—not teacher, preacher, or psychologist—has the same opportunity to mold minds, nurture bodies, and develop potential usefulness like a mother. It is both practical and consistent with the basic qualities that nature has given male and female that the woman who bears and nurses the baby should cart for the young and for the dwelling in which the young live. Though a woman [in] the twenty-first century is different in many ways from her foremothers, she is in at least one-way forever the same. Some would say that she is a servant of her biological fate, to which she has to adjust her other pursuits, Of course, this may be interpreted as mere slavery with the procreative and nurturing tasks as the shackles; but, on the other hand, this biological duty may also be accepted as a divinely assigned destiny with the awesome opportunity for a woman to link hand and heart with the Creator God in bearing and preparing the next generation as the binding cord.

"I left Texas A&M for one reason. Mama called."

—Bear Bryant

MENTORING

o o o o o o o o o o o o o o o o o o o o o o o o o o o o o o o

"I have more understanding than all my mentors; for your testimonies are my meditation." Psalms 119:99

Bear Bryant was the perhaps the greatest student of the game in the fifties and sixties and Wilkinson was at ease playing the role of mentor. The two men often went to dinner with several others, but invariably would wind up sitting together at a distant table, hunkered over a legal pad, drawing up plays. Instead of simple Xs and Os, Wilkinson often brought along what he called the "little men," which were miniature wooden football players that were used to simulate formations.

As I see it, there are two kinds of mentoring: passive and active.

Passive teaching happens when a person learns simply by observation—whether or not it is realized by the 'mentor' that they are being watched. For example, a piano student may learn about hand positioning by going to a concert to hear and see a professional pianist.

Active mentoring occurs when there is a formal and understood relationship between the mentor and mentoree. An example of this is when the concert pianist teaches piano to her students. Or, even more so, when the same pianist takes a promising student to go on tour with her—not necessarily to perform, but to observe all that being a professional pianist entails.

A very important fact is that in order for mentoring to be effective it must be wanted and welcomed. The mentoree must desire to be mentored. I know a man for whom I don't have very much respect and yet who feels very free about offering me advice. Unfortunately, he doesn't seem concerned about whether or not the counsel is wanted.

Effective, godly mentoring is so very needed!

Who are your passive mentors?

Do you have one or more active mentors? Who are they? Who are some potential active mentors?

Are you living in a way in which you are an effective passive mentor?

Are you cautious and sensitive as to when, how and to whom you offer counsel?

"When folks are ignorant, you don't condemn them, you teach them."

—Bear Bryant

MILLION DOLLAR MUSIC

"And it came to pass as they came, when David was returned from the slaughter of the Philistine, that the women came out of all cities of Israel, singing and dancing, to meet King Saul, with drums, with joy, and with instruments of music."
1 Samuel 18:6

Coach Paul "Bear" Bryant used to mention that every time he was on the practice field and would hear the Million Dollar Band practicing "Yea Alabama", he got goose bumps every time.

During David's long nights, playing his harp, singing the songs he made up, he often thought and sang about God. He sang about God's love and protection of the people God had created. These people were to God like the sheep were to David. Many of the songs were about God and His love and protection of the people who are the sheep of God's pasture are in the book of Psalms, which means "songs" of praise and gratitude to the great God who created the whole universe and all of the animals and people upon the earth.

"I'm always humming those good Sunday school choruses, like 'Jesus Loves Me' and 'Love Lifted Me."

—Bear Bryant

MOUNTAIN TOP EXPERIENCE

"And after six days Jesus took with him Peter, and James, and John, and lead them up into an high mountain apart by themselves: and he was transfigured before them." Mark 9:2

Coach Paul William "Bear" Bryant ascended to the mountain top of major college football's win list (315) November 28, 1981 when his Bama squad rallied for a pair of touchdowns in a 28-17 win over Auburn. Bryant surpassed Amos Alonzo Stagg's previously unbreakable record of 314 wins. The Year of 315 was a season of intense national media coverage and pressure that was expected to lift Bryant even higher among coaching immortals. The 1981 team also featured a 13th and final SEC title for Bryant at Alabama.

This is the story of a "mountaintop experience" of Jesus by three of his Disciples. Jesus is "transfigured," that is, seen is as changed by glory; his clothes appeared as dazzling white, and the two great figures of Hebrew history appeared by him: Moses and Elijah (which may represent the "law and the prophets" testifying to Jesus as God's anointed one). The voice from the cloud is reminiscent of the voice at Jesus' baptism: "This is my Son, the Beloved," with the injunction, "listen to him." Peter wants to encapsulate the experience of glory by building a little tabernacle around the vision of glory. But mountaintop experiences are fleeting and cannot be captured in order to be re-experienced again and again. They are given by God and usually come when we least expect them; we cannot generate them or "hold onto them."

"I always called my home, Metropolitan Moro Bottom. I came a long ways after that."

—Bear Bryant

MOURNING

'And He led them out as far as Bethany, and He lifted up His hands and blessed them. And it came about that while He was blessing them, He parted from them. And they returned to Jerusalem with great joy, and were continually in the temple, praising God." Luke 24:50-53

Bear Bryant once said, "I'd probably croak in a week if I ever quit coaching," On January 26, 1983, just 37 days after he had coached his final football game, Paul William "Bear" Bryant died of a heart attack at the age of 69 and a state—along with a nation, for that matter—mourned.

Jesus had felt the pain you and I feel when we are separated by death from a friend. This is another instance where Jesus identified directly with us so He could know what we go through. Because of His willingness to live the life we live, He cannot rightly be called distant. He is intimately acquainted with us and our daily struggles to our deepest griefs, to our greatest joys. Thirty-three years prior, Jesus had left the splendor of Heaven. Able to clothe Himself in pure light and glory if He so desired at His whim. He left it all to be born of a poor, virgin girl. He lived in a foreign country for the first several years of his life. He learned His stepfather's trade. It seems likely that Joseph died before Jesus was age 30.

During His three-year ministry, He demonstrated His power and authority over demons and sicknesses that were feared and misunderstood. He gave the people hope again, that God was not a book of rules but wanted to be a Father to them. He had been lauded and praised;

ridiculed, misrepresented and scorned. He had been turned over to be executed by the very people He had come to serve and to save as their Messiah—in obedience to the will of the Father. For one terrible moment in time, the Father had turned His back on Jesus as He bore our sins upon the cross. He had been born to die and rise again to defeat death and sin. The outcome was not in question, but it came at a terrible cost, which only He could pay. Because of His sacrifice, we are free.

> *"Today we Americans lost a hero who always seemed larger than life. He was a hard, but loved taskmaster. Patriotic to the core, devoted to his players, and inspired by a winning spirit that would not quit. Bear Bryant gave his country the gift of life unsurpassed. In making the impossible seem easy, he lived what we strive for."*
>
> —Ronald Reagan, U.S. President on Bear's death

NARROW DEFEATS

"Narrow is the way which leads to life and there are few who find it." Matthew 7:14

It is a mark of greatness in football when accomplishments are measured as much in narrow defeat as in triumphant victory.

In 1958, Bryant lost four games by a total of 25 points.
In 1959, he lost two games by a total of 21 points
In 1960, he lost one game by 13 points
In 1962, he lost one game by 1 point
In 1963, he lost two games by a total of 6 points
In 1964, he lost one game by 4 points
In 1967, he lost two games by a total of 15 points
In 1968, he lost three games by a total of 28 points
In 1971, he lost one game by 32 points
In 1972, he lost two games by a total of 5 points
In 1973, he lost one game by 1 point
In 1974, he lost one game by 2 points
In 1975, he lost one game by 13 points
In 1976, he lost three games by a total of 27 points
In 1977, he lost one game by 7 points
In 1978, he lost one game by 10 points
In 1980, he lost two games by a total of 10 points
In 1981, he lost two games by a total of 7 points
In 1982, he lost four games by a total of 27 points

We often look at defeat as a terrible thing. The world will go to any lengths to get what it wants—lie, cheat, steal. But, when a Christian does the best they can, and still loses, they still have won the victory. It takes a strong person to face defeat without getting upset, and taking revenge. Their faith wasn't shaken; they will be out there playing just as hard next weekend, ready to take on the world! We must, by God's example, overcome the world, or it will overcome us with ruin.

*"I firmly believe that if I had done a **better job**, we wouldn't have lost at Texas A&M. We were losing **games by three and four and six points.**"*

—Bear Bryant

NEW CLOTHES

"And why take thought for your clothes? Consider the lilies of the field, how they grow; they toil not, neither do they spin. And I say to you, that even Solomon in all his glory was not dressed like one of these. Therefore, if God so clothes the grass of the field, which today is and tomorrow is cast into the oven, shall he not much more clothe you, Oh you of little faith? Mathew 6:28-30

Bear's wardrobe as a boy consisted of some overalls and hand me downs. When his family moved to Fordyce, his Mama bought him some khaki britches and a khaki shirt and for the first time in life he was dressed up. One Saturday in Fordyce his Mama took Bear into May's General Store and bought him a new pair of shoes. The man said," Do they fit?" Bear said, "Oh, yeah." They hurt his feet so bad he still had bunions and corns they raised until he died. One time he took off his shoes in church, just to get some relief, and either his Mama saw him or smelled him but afterward she sure whipped him.

Daniel wasn't impressed with the position of power, the noble attire or impressive jewelry. When you are walking in Godly influence, authority and power, man made power, dress and jewelry isn't all that meaningful anymore. In fact he says, "Keep your gifts for yourself or give your rewards to someone else; however, I will read the inscription to the king and make the interpretation known to him"(Daniel 5:17).

Does royalty, riches or rule attract you? Do you have to know the right people to feel good about yourself? Do you feel better about your-self when you are adorned with impressive jewelry? Come on, admit it!

Isn't easy to feel a little bit prideful, when you know you're all decked out in a new suit or a new dress and gold watch and polished shoes? It is alluring! Most people work they fingers to the bone to achieve a powerful position with the company. All that meant nothing to Daniel because he knew someone who had already clothed Him, who had already adorned him with influence, authority and power. If you are dependent upon things to make you feel good, your accounting is messed up. We are made significant through Christ living in us. Our position as Christians is we are joint heirs with Jesus Christ.

> *"Mama took those high top black shoes down to Mr. Clark, the shoemaker, and had him put some cleats on them. Boy, talk about proud! I wore those cleats to football, to class, to Sunday school."*
>
> —Bear Bryant

OLD GLORY

Four of five days out to sea, Bear's ship was rammed by another ship in the convoy. Put a hole in the U.S.S. Uruguay two hundred sixty feet long. Bear got as far up from the water as he could. There were soldiers all around him praying and he was leading them. The ship lay dead in the water about three days. Nobody slept. A German sub could have taken them with a pocketknife. Finally another ship came along and rescued them and took them back to Bermuda.

Tom and his sister Sonya sat on the curb watching the Fourth of July parade. "Here comes our school band," said Tom. "And look at Old Glory! Isn't she pretty?" said an elderly man who was sitting in a wheelchair. "Old Glory?" asked Tom. "He means the flag, silly!" Sonya said. "Old Glory is a name for the flag." The man nodded. "You two forgot to stand at attention as the flag passed by," he told them. "But almost no one does that," protested Sonya. "No," agreed the man, "only a few. I imagine they're the ones who know the price of that flag." "Price? Did that flag cost more than other flags?" wondered Tom. "Is that a special flag?" "To me, my country's flag is always special," answered the old man. "If I could stand, I certainly would. I was wounded while fighting for that flag and for what it represents-all the blessings and freedoms God has given us in this country. He has given us a free nation, but there was a price to pay. I like to believe I'm in this wheelchair today so that the flag can go down the street. These other people who stood at attention probably fought for Old Glory, too-or know and love someone who has. They know how much it cost because they helped pay the price." "We're sorry," said Tom. "I guess we didn't realize what our freedom cost." "Many brave men and women gave their lives for that freedom," said the man, "and others-like me-were wounded. It's important to show proper respect for our flag and our country." "I think our flag and our freedom will mean more to us now," said Sonya. Do you stand at attention when the National Anthem is sung and the Pledge of Allegiance is said? Be sure to do that. As the Pledge of Allegiance says, it is "under God" that you have the liberties you enjoy. Thank God that you live in a country where He is recognized.

"All I had time to do was go home and kiss Mary Harmon hello and goodbye. The next day I was in Washington and shortly after in the U.S. Navy."

—Bear Bryant

ONE MAN

o o o o o o o o o o o o o o o o o o o o o o o o o o o o o o o
"For the body is not one member, but many." 1Corinthians
12:14

Joe Namath had a good season his junior year, although his rushing and passing stats were below those of his sophomore year. He hoped to have a superior game against Miami, the last game of the regular season. But after the previous week's loss to Auburn, Joe was seen breaking Bryant's strict training rules. (According to rumors, he had been drinking.) Bryant confronted Joe, and Joe admitted the transgression. In a press conference, Bryant announced he was suspending his star for the remainder of the season.

"I knew Joe wasn't a bad boy," Bryant later said. "I don't think he became bigheaded and felt he was above training rules. I don't think he ever was bigheaded—just always confident, and I like that. I feel if I'd done a good job of leadership, the suspension wouldn't have happened."

Joe accepted his punishment and watched as Steve Sloan led the team to wins over Miami, and Ole Miss in the Sugar Bowl.

We must be willing to delegate responsibilities to others who have the gifts and strengths to follow through within the task. We must be able to see those strengths and put them to use where they will be the most helpful, useful and profitable.

Churches that fail to grasp this concept will, sadly, begin to fall short of meeting the needs of their congregations. The God they serve has placed "within the body" plenty of people to get the things done that need to get done without pastors, staff members, and other "church employees" having to carry the entire load. Too many times, pastors feel they must be in control of ever aspect of ministry within the church. They hold onto a piece of every project that comes their way. They get involved in everything, and usually try to take the reins, even if someone else was leading the specific project. When one person is the only accepted authority, visionary and mouthpiece in any entity, then what was an organism becomes a giant head with no legs, arms, feet and hands. That's not a healthy body, it's a mutation—a monster. And you will soon find that nothing is getting done or if things are getting done, they all have the same goal and bent. Why? Because one person just can't do everything.

"One man doesn't make a team. It takes 11."

—Bear Bryant

PASS PLAY

o o o o o o o o o o o o o o o o o o o o o o o o o o o o o o o
"Commit thy way unto the LORD; trust also in him; and he
shall bring [it] to pass." Psalms 37:5

Though he had a reputation for running a conservative, ball control
offense, Bryant could also coach a passing team when he had the right
quarterback. With Vito "Babe" Parilli at quarterback in 1950, Kentucky set a record for touchdown passes with 27, and Bryant also had
fine passing teams with Namath and Ken "Snake" Stabler at Alabama.

We traveled almost 300 miles to play the state final. A mixture of
sleet and rain continued throughout the day, turning the playing field
into a muddy, icy mess. We fell behind early to a smaller, quicker team
that seemed better able to adapt. Desperate to catch up, we started
passing the ball in the sloppy conditions.

I had a miserable day, throwing five interceptions as we lost by two
touchdowns. The fairy tale I had been living came to an abrupt end.
There was no backslapping or hugging that day. I walked off the field
with my head down, alone in my misery.

Or so I thought.

Out of the corner of my eye I spied a figure keeping pace with me. I
turned to see Dad, who had hurried onto the field to walk me to our
locker room. It was a long walk. Though Dad said nothing, his actions
told me he would share my failures when nobody else would. I
wouldn't have to endure my pain alone.

I understood then why I hadn't seen Dad after the victories—I
didn't need him then, and he was content to watch from a distance.

But now, when I needed him, he was there. Though he didn't make the pain go away, he was willing to share it with me.

I believe a father's love is intended to mirror God's own selfless, perfect love for us. My dad has modeled the Father's love to me many times—but the time he met me in the end zone stands above the rest. It was a powerful reminder that the Lord, always present at our success, is also quick to draw near in times of trials and despair.

"Only three things can happen on a pass play and two of them are bad."

—Bear Bryant

PATRIOTISM

By 1958, at the age of 44 his reputation as a first rate football coach with a fiery temper and a love for God and country was well known. For the next twenty odd years, Paul "Bear" Bryant made a hounds tooth hat and a rolled up depth chart synonymous with winning football. His gravelly voice had nothing but compliments and praise for his opponents. He embodied the idea of sportsmanship and winning with class.

The United States of America was born on July 4, 1776. For some people, it was re-born on September 11, 2001.

Did you own a US flag prior to that infamous day last fall? Did you know all the words to "God Bless America" before it was sung in the seventh inning of every major league baseball game? It's okay if you decided to jump on board the patriotic bandwagon on September 12. This is the first time your love for your country is being truly tested. Four years ago, Peggy Noonan (former speechwriter for President Ronald Reagan) prophetically wondered, "In a coming crisis, down the road, will our children grown to adulthood have the thing within them that prompts them to protect their country?"

So what's this "thing" that you're supposed to have inside you? My dictionary defines patriotism as simply "love for or devotion to one's country." And if you love God, you're one step ahead of the pack.

The US allows its people to openly worship God; even to tell others about Him. (Christians in other countries have been arrested and imprisoned for doing as much—or less.) The founders of our country linked their patriotism with belief in the Creator. They declared that "all men are created equal" and that the Creator endowed mankind with "certain unalienable rights that among these are life, liberty, and the pursuit of happiness." And every time you pledge allegiance to the flag you recognize that the United States is "one nation, under God."

So what does patriotism mean to you? It's a question no one can answer for you, but one worth exploring in these uncertain times—no matter what country you call home. I urge you to learn more about how your country was founded and its place in the world today. Think about why God placed you here at this time in history and how you and your generation can make things better.

"If there was going to be a fight I want to be in it.'

—Bear Bryant, Dec. 7,1941

PAYING ATTENTION

o o o o o o o o o o o o o o o o o o o o o o o o o o o o o o
"My Son, attend to my words; incline thine ear unto my sayings." Proverbs 4:20

It was less than two weeks until the opening game of the season. Coaches were moving rapidly back and forth through the area, either barking out commands or totally immersed in the information on their clipboards. Not a single one of them even glanced at me. I didn't mind. For a lifelong Alabama/Bear Bryant fan, it was like finally making it to heaven.

I guess I had sat there for fifteen or twenty minutes. I was leafing through one of the previous year's game programs when there was an energy shift—I don't know any other way to describe it. I looked up as Coach Bryant walked into the office.

In a split second he surveyed the reception area, saw me, and realized I wasn't being attended to. He took off his cap and came over. I jumped up so quickly I almost fell on my face. He pretended not to notice. He stuck out a huge right hand, smiled almost shyly and said, "I'm Coach Bryant, can I help you?"

We talked for a half an hour and his eyes never left mine. There was no doubt in my mind but what I had his total attention. I sensed people moving around us—people who wanted to talk to 'The Man,' but no one interrupted. He didn't need the truck but he said he'd put us on the list of people who wanted to donate one. We shook hands again and as we did he said, "It's sure been good talking to you." I knew he meant it

I have always enjoyed listening to the conversations between adults. This is especially true when theological topics, or questions of practical religion, or questions of family culture, come up. I learn this way.

I hate taking notes. I hate it as much as I hate spelling. But I set myself to take notes on the teaching and conversation in church, or when I am listening to a special speaker. Taking notes forces me to focus on what is being said, and it allows me to review later what I have learned.

"I know I got a lot of attention for the way I did things at Kentucky and Texas A&M."

—Bear Bryant

PENALTIES

"How much more severely do you think a man deserves to be penalized who has trampled the Son of God under foot, who has treated as an unholy thing the blood of the covenant that sanctified him, and who has insulted the Spirit of grace?" Hebrews 10:29

Bear Bryant hated penalties and he was the first coach that used an official at practice every day to call any penalties. He wanted the officials to be picky about it too. He worked at avoiding penalties and he wanted total discipline on the field. No one was as conscious of avoiding penalties as Bryant was. It was just one of the many things he worked on that helped his teams win.

Secular people are increasingly coming to the conclusion that the best way to reduce crime in America is to make everything legal. They reason that laws are the problem, not the solution, and that more policemen, stiffer penalties, and no frills prison life only provoke the problem. Fewer_laws will work better they say. Spiritually speaking, many have come to the equal but opposite conclusion that in one's walk with God more laws will ensure a greater level of holy living. Both extremes could be called" legalism," but with dramatically differing emphases.

Spiritual legalism represents the opposite of license or lawlessness (a form of libertarianism or antinomianism) which overemphasizes one's liberty at the expense of obeying Scripture by reasoning that a Christian is free to act any way under grace without Divine restraint. While legalism and license are opposites, they both are extremely unscriptural. Christian liberty does not allow for license to sin, nor should genuine liberty be stifled by legalism. Christian obedience should not be infused with legalism nor diminished by license. Where biblical injunctions to obedience are clear and direct, obedience is always required by God. In certain life situations, where the Scriptures have not outlined a specific response, then Christian liberty should prevail. May God give us the wise discernment to steer a righteous course through life, following the navigational aids of Scripture, and never run aground on the shoal waters of either legalism or license.

"Coach Bryant was great at coaching players, coaching assistant coaches and coaching game officials."

—Clem Gryska, Alabama assistant coach

PERFECTIONIST

○ ○
"Be perfect, therefore, as your heavenly Father is perfect."
Matthew 5:48

Bear Bryant substituted every player who ever went into a game while he was coaching. The reason was that he knew how he wanted to play that game, with whom and how long. He also knew different coaches have different personalities and he wanted to control the personality of the team. He was that organized and that much of a perfectionist.

Striving for excellence isn't always a bad thing. Doing our best is part of the Christian life. We know our whole lives are offerings to God, and that we need to give God our best. We are supposed to shoot for the highest standard of goodness—God's goodness. But perfectionism is "doing our best" for all the wrong reasons. Perfectionism is about us, not about God. I was being good because I thought it would help me earn love and acceptance. If my behavior pleased my parents, they'd love me even more. If my behavior pleased God, I'd earn his favor. I came to believe my worth was based on how good I was—and on how good other people thought I was. Inside, I was stressed out. The pressure to be perfect was almost too much to handle. But I didn't think I could tell anyone how I felt because that would mean admitting I wasn't perfect. And that was the last thing I wanted to do. Perfectionism is a losing game. Fortunately, it's one we really don't have to play. After all, God reached out to us when we were as far away from him as we could possibly be. Being a Christian isn't about being perfect; it's about being forgiven. So we can relax and be confident that God knows we're not perfect and loves us just the same.

"I never claimed to be perfect or even a genius at the game of football."

—Bear Bryant

PLATEAU

o o o o o o o o o o o o o o o o o o o o o o o o o o o o o o o o
"We urge you, brethren, warn those who are idle, encourage
the timed, help the weak, be patient with everyone" 1 Thessalonians 5:14

Coach Bryant never reached a plateau. He would be named national
champion on a Monday night and he was back coaching early Tuesday
morning, working to win another one. A normal person would say,
"We've had a great year and we've done a good job, so I'm going to
have a great summer." But not him. He was never that way. He was
driven to succeed over and over. He worked just as hard after a 12-0
season as he worked after a 6-5 season. That is why there were not
many of those bad years. He was a strong leader who set a fast pace.
Everyone had to work hard with him just to keep up.

The Apostle Paul may not have had plateaued believers in mind
when he wrote his first Epistle to the Thessalonians. The key is understanding the different categories of need. Idle is a military term meaning 'to break ranks.' While the body of Messiah is marching forth in
service, they have deserted. For people in this category, who have with-
drawn from accountability, the solution is loving confrontation. Love
them and get in their face. The timid are those who are afraid to do
what God wants them to do. They have stopped growing because they
are resisting some issue of 'the will of God.' They need encouragement.
The Weak are physically sick or emotionally sick...Very often believers
plateau because of some traumatic experience in life that has nearly
destroyed them. We give them the support they need until their spiritual vitality is restored. And be patient covers everybody. If we are

131

going to get into this service, know that it's going to be hard. It's going to be draining. It's going to tax our resources. And if we try to pull out halfway through, we are going to make matters worse. Just as the problem of spiritual stagnation usually develops slowly, so the solution generally takes time. For the spirit, as well as the body, there are no miracle diets or instant fitness plans. True health comes through the simple things, and often it starts with the help of a friend. Nothing helps a plateaued believer as much as another concerned believer. Someone who says, 'You've been sitting on this ledge too long. You and I are going to climb together. And we're going to make it to the top.'

"If my 75% boy plays 15% over his ability and your 100% boy slogs around and plays 15% under his, then we will beat you every time."

—Bear Bryant

PLOWBOY

○ ○

"Give ye ear, and hear my voice; hearken, and hear my speech. Doth the plowman plow all day to sow? doth he open and break the clods of his ground? When he hath made plain the face thereof, doth he not cast abroad the fitches, and scatter the cummin, and cast in the principal wheat and the appointed barley and the rye in their place? For his God doth instruct him to discretion, and doth teach him. For the fitches are not threshed with a threshing instrument, neither is a cart wheel turned about upon the cummin; but the fitches are beaten out with a staff, and the cummin with a rod. Bread corn is bruised; because he will not ever be threshing it, nor break it with the wheel of his cart, nor bruise it with his horsemen. This also cometh forth from the LORD of hosts, which is wonderful in counsel, and excellent in working." Isaiah 28:23-29

Paul William Bryant was born a place near Fordyce, Arkansas called Morro Bottom on September 11, 1913. Born the eleventh of twelve children, his family was poor and worked hard to eak out a meager existence. Young Paul Bryant quickly found himself behind a plow every morning before school and then back behind it again until sunset. On the weekends, both he and his mother would drive a mule and wagon to the nearby town of Fordyce to sell produce.

Isaiah gives us a very good piece of wisdom and he gives it to us in a manner that is devised to make us think for ourselves. Does the farmer plow continually to plant seed? Does he continually turn and harrow the ground? Well, does a farmer do this? Does a farmer continually plow from early spring until late fall? Of course he doesn't, or there would never be any crop. This is simple common sense; yet all too often, we fail to use this God given Common sense. Think about this as we return to Isaiah's example of the farmer. Does he not level its surface, and sow dill and scatter cumin, And plant wheat in rows, Barley in its place, and rye within its area? Sometimes we complicate things in our lives too much. We always are plowing things up. We never stop long enough to level the surface, and to plant seed. And we have to be even more patient with the things in our lives, or we will never get the results we desire, just as the farmer must wait for the crops to mature. This is simple wisdom.

> *"I'm just a simple plowhand from Arkansas, but I have learned over the years how to hold a team together. How to lift some men up, how to calm others down, until finally they've got one heartbeat, together, a team."*

—Bear Bryant

POLITICS

ooooooooooooooooooooooooooooooooooooo

"As for King Zedekiah of Judah, the politicians around him, and the rest of the people of Jerusalem who have stayed in this land or moved to Egypt—I, the Lord, will treat them all like these figs that are too bad to be eaten." Jeremiah 24:8

When Bear Bryant was at the top of his game, there was speculation the football coach would run for governor of the state of Alabama.

George Wallace, a man with a vested interest in such a power play, questioned why Bryant would allow himself to be pulled by the political tide. "Why would he want the second most popular job in the state?" Wallace quipped. Bryant was viewed as the god of football and, more or less, king of Alabama.

Politics weaves its way through our daily lives altering events great and small. From seat belts to national security, every level of governmental politics has something to say about almost everything and everyone. In my state it is illegal to ride a motorcycle without a helmet, or drive a car or be a front seat passenger without a seat belt. You can be ticketed for any of these acts, much to the consternation of personal freedom groups.

Jesus' arrest, trial and execution were all politically motivated. Even more, politics could not cease the grinding wheels of the Jerusalem Council—the Sanhedrin. The Roman guard placed at the tomb was won with a little political arm-twisting. A 16-man unit of soldiers was probably dispatched to the garden tomb. The guards were a political barrier against a political trump card that might be played by the disciples.

It is not hard at all to see the parallels today in political arenas around the world and across the street. The motivation for self is the hardest thing to deny, and sometimes hardest to see. Even some of our very best acts, which help others, are motivated by selfishness. Realizing this is not easy, but it an important step in shedding the old man—the old human nature to be replaced by Jesus' nature in our hearts and minds.

> *"The great state of Alabama casts 1 1/2 votes for Bear Bryant for president."*
>
> —1968 Democratic convention chairman on the first ballot

POOR

o o o o o o o o o o o o o o o o o o o o o o o o o o o o o o o o o

For if you give, you will get! Your gift will return to you in
full and overflowing measure, pressed down, shaken together
to make room for more, and running over. Whatever measure you use to give—large or small—will be used to measure
what is given back to you." (Luke 6:38)

For most college players, the ultimate goal is to be recruited by a professional football team. For John Coyle that created a problem for as
long as he could remember, his dream had been to create a ranch for
homeless boys. Just before graduation he went to Coach Bryant and
said, "Coach, if I go to the pros and play four or five years I can probably make enough money to start the boy's ranch, what do you think?"
Coach Bryant said, "John, don't ever do anything you don't totally
believe in—don't do anything you aren't totally dedicated to. You
believe in that dream of yours. Forget the pros. Go build the
ranch...and John, if you do that, I'll do everything I can to help you."
After 'The Man' died, our business manager did some checking and
found that Coach Bryant had personally given over $80,000.00 to the
ranch and there is no way to know how much others gave that he was
directly responsible for. In fact at his last game, a fan tossed Bear a tee
shirt and said, "Coach if you'll autograph that, "I'll send $1,000.00 to
your favorite charity." As he signed the shirt, Coach Bryant said to the
man, 'send it to John Croyle at Big Oak Boy's Ranch.' " John Croyle
has "raised" over 1,600 kids. His success has been nothing short of
phenomenal. He attributes a lot of it to Coach Paul "Bear" Bryant.

If you bring all of your awareness into the moment, while living from love and eliminating ego, one day you will find that you too have become a legend and…that won't matter at all. Each of us has something to offer to someone in need. We can give our money and our time to charity, be a friend to someone who is sick or lonely, do volunteer work, or be a peacemaker. We may give unselfishly of our time to our spouse, children or parents. We may choose a service-oriented occupation, or we may just do our everyday jobs with integrity and respect for others. It would seem that the more we give to others, the poorer we become, but just the opposite is true! Service to others brings meaning and fulfillment to our lives in a way that wealth, power, possessions and self-centered pursuits can never match.

"Don't do anything you don't believe in"

—Bear Bryant

POPULARITY

"But from those recognized as important (what they really were makes no difference to me; God does not show favoritism)—those recognized as important added nothing to me."
Galatians 2:6

Kentucky was a basketball school lead by legendary basketball coach Adolph Rupp, and football was beginning to rival basketball in popularity. Rupp wanted Kentucky basketball to be number one, and Bryant wanted Kentucky football to be number one. Something had to give. During a Kentucky sports banquet, after both teams won the conference championship, the university presented Rupp with a brand new Cadillac and presented Bryant with a brand new cigarette lighter. Bear knew it was time to move on.

Sometimes Christians almost seem to try to be unpopular by being irritating by acting in a self-righteous way. How can you tell if the reason for your unpopularity is pleasing or not pleasing to God?

(God's children will always want to give glory to God, not to call attention to themselves. In all that we do, we want to lead others to Jesus, not to be irritating or give an impression of "better than thou." Rather, in humble obedience we serve the Savior by doing and saying what is according to his will.)

One day all who believe in him as the Savior will live with him eternally in heaven. Till then we can expect to be unpopular and even hated by those who don't know him as the Savior from sin. This would be very difficult for us if we had to rely on ourselves, but Jesus has promised to be with us. He asks the Father to send his Spirit to strengthen our faith so that we can serve, obey, and glorify him.

> *"Don't worry about winning popularity contests with your staff. You'd better worry about being respected. Anybody can be liked, a heck of a lot fewer respected."*

> —Bear Bryant

PRAYER

"And all things, whatever you ask for in prayer, believing, you will receive." Matthew 21:22

Bear Bryant never made a lot of noise about his faith, but it was important to him, He called it his belief. He read in President Truman's book where he said when you hear those loud prayers and they are louder than usual, you had better go home and lock up your silver. Bear didn't feel that way, of course, but he didn't think you needed to go around beating your breast either.

"Tell me about praying, Kirk."

"Well, it is just talking to God. I tell him everything. He is interested in everything I do. He listens when it is good and he listens when it is bad. It makes me feel good to talk to God. He is always right there, always by my side. I can feel him in my soul."

"When do you pray, Kirk?"

"That's easy, I pray when I need to...all the time! God answers my prayers, too!"

I delved a little more, "Does God always fix things for you?"

"Well, I don't always ask God for things, but he always answers my prayers."

"Kirk, I have to tell you, I am not always sure that God answers my prayers—sometimes it just feels like that, anyway."

"He answers your prayers; you just have to learn to listen...sometimes It's not what you want." That was the answer...I pray, I pray a lot, but I'm not a very good listener. Kirk, who tells God everything, has learned that listening is just as important as praying. Kirk has

141

Down syndrome. He has learned to love and trust in the purest and truest ways. He is always able to see things as they are, and his heart is always open. His vision is never clouded by the "stuff" that gets in the way for the rest of us.

"Some of the most tender and thankful sincere prayers I have ever heard were prayed in an athletic setting by Paul Bryant."

—Jim Goostree, Assistant AD

PRIDE

"I tell you that this man, rather than the other, went home justified before God. For everyone who exalts himself will be humbled, and he who humbles himself will be exalted." Luke 18:14

Let the Swanee Tiger scratch,
Let the Yellow Jacket sting,
Let the Georgia Bulldog bite,
Alabama still is right!
And whether win or lose we smile,
For that's Bama's fighting style:
You're Dixie's football PRIDE, Crimson Tide!
A-L-A-B-A-M-A
Yea Alabama! Drown 'em Tide.
Every Bama fan's behind you, hit your stride.
Go teach the Bulldogs to behave,
Send the Yellow Jackets to a watery grave.
And if a man starts to weaken,
That's his shame.
For Bama's pluck and grit have writ her name in Crimson flame.
Fight on, fight on, fight on men.
Remember the Rose Bowl, we'll win then.
Go roll to vict'ry, hit your stride.
You're Dixie's football pride, Crimson Tide!
My roots are in Alabama's sod,
I'm Southern by the Grace of God,

"Bear" Bryant taught me the meaning of pride,
My pledge of allegiance is ROLL TIDE!"
Does the Bible teach that we are to just think of ourselves at trash? Hardly. Rather that having too high (which is often the case in the world) or two low a self image (which is often the case in Christian circles) we are taught to have a proper self image knowing that we were sinners yet that Christ has set us free and changed us from the inside out, and that His strength is perfected in our weakness. Jesus was hard on those who thought too highly of themselves (the proud) and easy on those who knew they needed help.

> *"There is no way to describe the pride an Alabama player feels in himself and the tradition of the school."*
>
> —Kenny Stabler on tradition at the Capstone

PUNISHMENT

○ ○
"He who covers his sins will not prosper, but whoever confesses and forsakes them will have mercy." Proverbs 28:13

Joe had another good season his junior year, although his rushing and passing stats were below those of his sophomore year. He hoped to have a superior game against Miami, the last game of the regular season. But after the previous week's loss to Auburn, Joe was seen breaking Bryant's strict training rules. (According to rumors, he had been drinking.) Bryant confronted Joe, and Joe admitted the transgression. In a press conference, Bryant announced he was suspending his star for the remainder of the season.

How can you know if the Spirit or the flesh is leading you? Very simple: Look at your behavior.

What do you do when you discover you are not walking by the Spirit? Acknowledge it for what it is. You have consciously or unconsciously chosen to live independently of God by walking according to the flesh. Walking according to the Spirit is a moment-by-moment, day-by-day experience. Acknowledge your sin to God, seek the forgiveness of anyone you may have offended, receive forgiveness, and be filled with the Spirit.

"I knew Joe wasn't a bad boy, I don't think he became bigheaded and felt he was above training rules. I don't think he ever was bigheaded—just always confident, and I like that. I feel if I'd done a good job of leadership, the suspension wouldn't have happened."

—Bear Bryant

QUITTING

"Oh, that I had in the wilderness a lodging place for wayfaring men; that I might leave my people, and go from them."
Jeremiah 9:2.

It was a short-lived tenure at Maryland. Coach Bryant got into a dispute with President Byrd after he fired one of his assistants without telling him and reinstated a player Bryant had kicked off the team. Bryant knew he must quit. While looking though a stack of telegrams that evening, he noticed one offering him the head coaching job at Kentucky.

Many good people feel, and have felt like quitting at times. My guess is that most of us at one time or another have felt like Jeremiah and have wished for a little cabin in the mountains where we could "get away from it all" and rest. It may surprise you to learn that even Jesus felt like quitting. Just prior to His crucifixion He prayed, "O My Father, if it is possible, let this cup pass from Me." (Matt. 26:39b; cf. Heb. 12:3). If the Lord could feel like quitting and yet, not be guilty of sin (Heb. 4:15), I am confident that it is not wrong for you to feel the same way.

Remember—actually quitting would affect your service to God as well as your family. The Bible urges, "And let us not grow weary in well doing, for in due season we shall reap if we do not lose heart" Gal. 6:9

Feelings must dictate or control our behaviors, but we can't ignore our feelings either. They won't be ignored. Our feelings are very important. They count.

"Never quit. It is the easiest cop out in the world. Set a goal and don't quit until you attain it. When you attain it, set another goal, and don't quit until you reach it. Never quit."

—Bear Bryant

RECRUITING

"So the last shall be first, and the first last: for many be called,
but few chosen." Matthew 20:16

Bear Bryant believed there were no tricks to recruiting, just a matter of
seeing a boy and seeing him again, and you keep seeing him until you
win him. When you get down to it its wrong, because the boy ought to
go where he pleases and he shouldn't have a bunch of slick talking
salesmen influencing his life or selling him something he doesn't want.
If a boy wants to go to auburn he should go there. If he wants to go to
Alabama, the same thing. Recruiting was a challenge to Bear Bryant.

Kingdom of God is like a professional sports team on strike. The
field should be full of top-notch athletes, but instead it consists of second-rate amateurs who have been sent as replacements. For whatever
reason, the professionals who should be on the field have refused to
appear, leaving a sorry lot of substitutes to play in their place.

Nevertheless, the work of the Kingdom must continue, with or
without the help of professionals. God is pleased to call in the "second-
string" players on His team. He delights in using those who might
seem weak in every other respect. His name is glorified by ordinary
people who can't sing, can't write, or can't teach. You see, we've missed
the point of it all. Service to the Kingdom of God is not about perfect-
ing abilities or discovering some hidden "spiritual gift." It is first and
foremost about people who are willing to serve. It is about people who
desire to glorify God. What a relief it is when we come to the realization that God is glorified in our weaknesses. The sermon doesn't have
to be interesting, the newsletter riveting, or the music performed to

perfection. God is glorified by the faithfulness of His people. For those who are faithful, it matters little as to whether they are skilled. Perhaps you are a "professional" who has been on strike; or perhaps you're a second-rate substitute with no particular skills. The work of the Kingdom must go on. The Kingdom is recruiting all kinds of believers—young, old, working, retired, single, married, skilled and unskilled. There is no discrimination, no entrance requirement, and no prerequisite. The call to serve is given to all those who are willing to accept it. Will you?

"The thing about recruiting is that you have to learn—and learn fast—that you can't make the chicken salad without the chicken."

—Bear Bryant

RED SEA

"And Moses stretched out his hand over the Red Sea; and the Lord caused the water to divide." Exodus 14:21

There was a time one late evening when Bear came looking for one of his players who was out past curfew. It was a college nightspot, when the crowd parted like the Red Sea and through came Coach Paul "Bear" Bryant, directing himself to several Tide players in the wrong place at the wrong time. He spoke firm and loud to the players ~ "You need get to where you belong now and if you want to be somewhere this time of night, it should be in my living room where I can keep a eye on you!

There was silence for a moment, and the players took off with apologies directed to Coach Paul "Bear" Bryant. That was 1980, and I will never forget those years being a part of his era. He was not only a great college football coach, but also a mentor; a friend and someone who was always inspiring those around him to do their best in life...Win! No matter what the cause is.

God's power is revealed in so many ways. No one but God could part a sea. God also does many powerful things for us every day. He brings the sun up in the morning, he showers the earth with rain and makes the trees grow. He even created gravity to keep us from accidentally flying into outer space. This week, everyone should spend some time in prayer, thanking God for his mighty power.

"Coach Bryant couldn't control the weather, obviously, but he took charge while showing our players how to deal with it."

—Jim Goosetree, Alabama trainer

REDBUGS

o o o o o o o o o o o o o o o o o o o o o o o o o o o o o o
"He gave also their increase unto the caterpillars, and their labor unto the bugs." Psalms 78:46

Patrick May recommended the mascot of Fordyce High School, which, by the way, is the alma mater of Paul "Bear" Bryant. According to May, the school received this mascot in the 1920s when the football team played a game on a field that hadn't been mowed during the previous week. After the teams played on this chigger-infested football field, the players were covered in bug bites, and the school had a new mascot.

As Janie turned over a rock in the back yard, she drew back. "Yuck! Look at all the icky bugs hiding under this rock, Mom!" she exclaimed. "They look like they're wearing armor." Mother watched the bugs scurry around. "Those are sow bugs—or pill bugs," she said.

"They don't seem to like the sun. I think they're looking for a dark place to hide," observed Janie. "They're a little like us then, aren't they," Mother said thoughtfully.

Janie glanced at her mother in surprise. "What do you mean?"

"Well, just as these bugs are scrambling for hiding places, we sometimes scramble to find hiding places for the sin in our hearts," explained Mother. "We try to keep it in the dark, but God sees it."

"My Sunday school teacher was talking about sin last week. She says there are two kinds—there are sins of 'c-com-commission' and sins of 'omission.' " Janie was rather pleased with herself as she used the big words. "And do you know what that means?" asked Mother with a smile.

"The sins of 'commission' are the sins we commit—the bad things we think or do," answered Janie. "Like…its sin to fight, or lie, or say something to hurt somebody." "That's exactly right!" Mother nodded. "And what are the sins of 'omission'?" "That's when we don't do things we should do," answered Janie, "like not calling a friend when we know she's sad, or not telling a friend about Jesus when we get the chance."

"Good for you!" Mother smiled. "You remembered that lesson very well."

Janie nodded as she watched the last of the insects disappear. "I'll think of these guys as 'sin bugs' from now on," she said. She shuddered. "They'll be a reminder that I don't want sin in my heart."

"From the time he started playing football at Fordyce High School, every newspaper clipping said Bryant this and Bryant that."

—Collins Kilgore, cousin

REFINING

"And I will bring the third part through the fire, and will refine them as silver is refined, and will try them as gold is tried: they shall call on my name, and I will hear them: I will say, It is my people: and they shall say, The LORD is my God." Zechariah 13:9

Bear Bryant turned the Kentucky Wildcats into winners immediately, going 7-3 his first year. His reputation for being brilliant at refining offenses and defenses was starting to form. He lead the Wildcats to their only SEC title in 1950 with a 11-1 record and capped it with an upset over Oklahoma in the Sugar Bowl, snapping their 31 game winning streak. The following year, he added a Cotton Bowl win over TCU. In eight seasons Bryant took Kentucky to four bowls and soon became recognized as one of the brightest young coaches in the country.

The process of refining is a costly and time-consuming process. Refining gold is not simple. It takes time and intense heat. Our faith is far more valuable than gold. So the refining process will not be simple, but what it produces will be worth all the effort. If the refining process is necessary to prove our faith and to prepare us for the tasks we were created to do, how should we react to "speed bumps" in our lives?

When the disciple has worked through difficult times, his/her faith and character is refined for the doing of more powerful goodness in this hurting world. The Bible calls this God's "refining fire" in which the trash of life is burned up so the purer "gold" of our character before God remains. Out of the furnace of life's trouble, if the disciple continues to walk with Jesus and be formed by forgiveness and mercy, goodness becomes more abundant and love overflows to many more. This is where heaven shines more clearly on earth in the lives of disciples who have become apostles and leaders, mature and able to disciple other new apprentices of Jesus.

> *"It was a defense like none of us had ever seen. It didn't make sense to us. But when we got on the playing field with Oklahoma, the lights came on in our heads. They hadn't seen anything like it either and we shut them down."*
>
> —Ben Zaranka, Kentucky end on the Sugar Bowl win.

REMEMBERING THE IMPORTANT

o o o o o o o o o o o o o o o o o o o o o o o o o o o o o o
"And they remembered his words." Luke 24:8

During an interview before Bear Bryant's 200th win in 1971, he was asked about the big games during his career. He recalled about 35 games and talked about them, including reciting scores all the way back to the 1945 season at Maryland. When he finished the interview, he suggested the reporter check the scores of the games and when the reporter checked Bear had missed only one score by one point and that was a Kentucky game back about 1950. That was typical of him. He never forgot a single detail about anything and that was one of the things that made him unique and such a great coach.

Bible memorization is a strategic way to "renew your mind" You may be thinking, "but I don't have a good memory..." I admit some people have extra-ordinary potential to commit things to memory

We may be inclined to conclude that memory work is out of our reach. Instead, we should realize the potential God has given us. How many people who claim to be unskilled at memorizing can recite all kinds of facts about their favorite sport team's players and statistics? How many can recall details of books they have read, movies they have seen, conversations they have had? In other words, strategic Bible memory IS within the reach of everyone who chooses to VALUE IT!

When we memorize and meditate on strategic verses, we are blessed with stronger faith. Have you ever been plagued by troublesome memories that are hard to shake? You try to put your mind elsewhere, but the negative thoughts zip back like a boomerang? The key to getting out of this rut—you guessed it—is to memorize and meditate on God's written truth.

What verse of Scripture has had an impact in your heart lately? Why not commit it to memory this week? Enjoy the insights of meditation and share the Word during times of fellowship and witnessing.

> *"When people ask me what do I want to be remembered for, I have only one answer: I want people to remember me as a winner."*
>
> —Bear Bryant

REPLACING A LEGEND

o o o o o o o o o o o o o o o o o o o o o o o o o o o o o o
"And they gave forth their lots; and the lot fell upon Matthias; and he was numbered with the eleven apostles" Acts 1:26

If you want some insight into replacing a legend, call Ray Perkins. He succeeded Bear Bryant. Alabama has had five coaches since Bryant resigned at the end of the 1982 season. It even won a national championship with Gene Stallings in 1992. But it has never replaced the Bear. Alabama might hire another a good coach. It might even hire another great coach. But it won't replace Bear. Bear didn't just win national championships and SEC titles; he won with flair and controversy. He won with a hounds tooth hat and a weathered face. He didn't just win. He entertained. He changed the face of SEC football along the way. In fact, he had more impact on this SEC than anyone. After Alabama went 6-4 and 6-5 in 1969-70, Bryant switched to the wishbone offense. The Tide only lost one SEC game in the next five years. While Bryant converted Alabama to the option, he didn't take the rest of the league with him. The Vols, Tigers, Gators and everybody else basically kept doing what they were doing.

This is the only instance in the New Testament where Christians are said to have "cast lots" in order to make a choice. This particular choice involved a very important question: Which of two apparently equally qualified men should be selected to take Judas' place among the twelve apostles? It is significant that before the lots were cast, they all prayed and asked the Lord to indicate His choice (Acts 1:24)

In any case, it is important to note that the Bible's single mention of this practice by Christians indicates that it was preceded by earnest prayer for the Lord to reveal His will, not merely the preference of the one voting. We also always should seek earnestly the Lord's leading in any choice we are called on to make in any election.

> *"I think Bebes (Stallings) will do an excellent job keeping the what we have built here at the university."*

> —Bear Bryant

RESPECT FOR THE DEAD

"Show family affection to one another with brotherly love.
Outdo one another in showing honor." Romans 12:10

At Bear Bryant's funeral, so many people showed up that they filled three churches in downtown Tuscaloosa. The five-mile procession slowly rolled down Tenth Street, past the stadium that for twenty-four years had been filled with fans cheering him on, past Memorial Coliseum where his office was located. Then the somber caravan made its way to I-59, where all traffic stopped to allow its passage. Officials estimated between one-half and one million people lined the fifty-three mile stretch to Elmwood Cemetery in Birmingham, just blocks away from Legion Field.

Respect for the dead isn't what it used to be. In days long gone, mourners would gather in a country church for a funeral service to say farewell to loved ones. Then, the casket would be loaded on a wagon, and mourners would follow behind on a sad walk to the cemetery, usually adjacent to the church. But eventually, horse-drawn wagons became motorized hearses. Mourners rode behind long black cars in limousines. And the processions grew as more and more people bought their own cars.

It has been tradition for at least the past half-century for cars on both sides of the road to pull over in respect for the dead as funeral processions pass by.

Stopping for a funeral procession is not only a southern tradition, but it is a display of respect by passing motorists for the family that has lost a loved one. It is not a time to discover how fast your vehicle can go when you hit the gas to zip around the line of slow moving cars.

The act of pulling over for a procession brings a sense of thankfulness and pride to those riding in the black limousine. It shows that we as community members, neighbors, friends and fellow Americans can take a few minutes of our time to share with the family members a feeling of loss. It usually makes the motorist a bit nostalgic.

Have some respect, folks. If you've been the person in the procession, you know how it feels to see motorists pull over.

Let's continue this courteous tradition for our fellow community members. Remember, if you haven't been in the procession, one day you will.

> *"It is difficult, if not impossible, to put into words what the entire funeral scene meant to me. It was a monument to his greatness."*
>
> —Jim Goostree, Alabama associate athletics director

REVITALIZED

o o o o o o o o o o o o o o o o o o o o o o o o o o o o o o o o o o
"Then said Samuel to the people, Come, and let us go to Gil-
gal, and revitalize the kingdom there." 1 Samuel 11:14

While recruiting his first class at Alabama, Bryant told his freshmen
that if they followed his rules and played they way he demanded, they
would win the National Championship before they graduated. Many
thought Bryant's statement as just another recruiting tactic.

But Bryant turned the program around almost instantly, going 5-4-
1. That was more games than Bama had won in the previous 36. His
second squad went 7-2-2 and earned a trip to the Liberty Bowl. In
1961, with the help of players like Trammell, Jordan, and Neighbors,
Bama went 11-0 and won the National Championship after beating
Arkansas in the Sugar Bowl. Bryant's earlier promise to his then freshmen proved accurate. It was the Crimson Tide's sixth National Championship and Bryant's first at the Capstone. In only four years, Paul
"Bear" Bryant had revitalized the Crimson Tide football program into
the nation's top-ranked college football team once again.

WHAT DOES IT MEAN TO BE A REVITALIZED PART OF
THE BODY OF CHRIST? TO BE ALIVE AGAIN, FILLED WITH
THE POWER OF THE HOLY SPIRIT, AWAKENED,
RENEWED, SEEKING GOD'S WILL FOR ME, FOR YOU, FOR
US, IN ALL THINGS. TO KNOW GOD...NOT JUST WITH
OUR MINDS, BUT IN OUR HEARTS...IN THE VERY DEPTHS
OF OUR SOULS, HIS COMPASSION, LOVE, FORGIVENESS,
MERCY. ALLOWING THE FIRE OF THE HOLY SPIRIT TO
FLAME THE EMBERS OF OUR HEARTS, ALLOWING THE

FLAME TO BE IGNITED THAT CANNOT BE QUENCHED. SHARING IT WITH THE WORLD, THE GOOD NEWS OF JESUS CHRIST! GOD IS WITH US YESTERDAY, TODAY, AND TOMORROW. GOD LOVES US, FORGIVES US, IS MERCI-FUL, AND SEEKS COMMUNION WITH US, THROUGH HIS SON JESUS CHRIST! SHOUT IT FROM THE ROOFTOPS! GOD IS WITH US, WE ARE NOT ALONE, PRAISE BE TO GOD!

"All my life I have wanted to come back here and live."

—Mary Harmon Bryant, on their return to Alabama

RIGHT STUFF

○ ○

"Who is the image of the invisible God, the firstborn of every creature."? Colossians 1:15

Coach Paul "Bear" Bryant. The name was an inspiration in itself, conjuring images of a man in a hounds tooth hat standing by the goal post, coaching his team to yet another victory. Years of experience were etched in his gentle face, but behind the grandfatherly exterior lay what could 'be described as the right stuff, the stuff that created a legend.

The phrase "Essence of God" is a theological term used to refer to God's personal characteristics, or to the facets of His personality. Sometimes the term "Attributes of God" is used to refer to God's essence. The "attributes", or the "essence", of God are His primary characteristics, so they cannot be completely communicated to man. They can be described to a degree, but they cannot be fully defined.

Finite man cannot define the infinite. The Bible is the Word of God, and as such it reveals those facts about the Creator that He has seen fit to reveal about Himself.

All of the characteristics of the divine essence are present in God at all times, but not all are manifest at the same time, just as while all colors are present in a ray of white light, the individual colors can be seen only under certain conditions of reflection or refraction.

All of the characteristics of the divine essence are present in God at all times, but not all are manifest at the same time, just as while all colors are present in a ray of white light, the individual colors can be seen only under certain conditions of reflection or refraction.

"If you don't have the talent to win with talent alone, you have to compensate."

—Bear Bryant

RULES

○ ○
"And if a man also competes as an athlete, yet is he not crowned, except he competes by the rules." 2 Timothy 2:5

When Bear came to Alabama in 1958, he told the people there, he wouldn't cheat, that he wouldn't violate the rules or let anybody else do it and he'd adhere to the spirit of the rules. He inherited one boy who some of the alumni were paying and he put a stop to it.

Bear didn't know hwy cheating had gotten so bad again in the 1970s unless it's a product of all that was read about on the front page or inflation.

In football's early years, you weren't allowed to throw a forward pass.

Rules and guidelines change in both sports and life. Activities that used to be considered off-limits for Christians have become acceptable. I could fill you in on the details about changes in rules and standards toward movies, music, and other forms of entertainment.

Some rules are necessary to give guidance, but we also need to realize that even if what we call "rules" or "guidelines" have changed, the Guidebook has never changed at all.

The unchangeable guidelines of the Bible give us enough to go on in making our entertainment decisions. We can test the value of a questionable event with these questions:

* Does it mean that I am not avoiding evil?
* Does it have a wholesome atmosphere?
* Will it hinder me in my walk with the Lord?

* Is it an offense to others?
* Is sexual immorality accepted or condoned?
* Can this activity be done to God's glory?
* Am I using my freedom to indulge in sin?
* Does it promote acts of the sinful nature?

Man-made rules change or are eliminated, and not always for the best reasons. That's why we need to depend on God's guidelines. If we face them honestly and ask ourselves the hard questions, we'll know what to do—no matter what the situation.

> *"My Three Rules for coaching: 1) Surround yourself with people who can't live without football. 2) Recognize winners. They come In all forms. 3) Have a plan for everything."*
>
> —Bear Bryant

RUNNING FOR YOUR LIFE

o o o o o o o o o o o o o o o o o o o o o o o o o o o o o
"I run to reach the end of the race and receive the prize for
which God, through Christ Jesus, is calling us up to heaven"
Philippians 3:14

In one game Alabama was ahead by just six points, and the clock had
less than two minutes to run. He sent this quarterback in with the
instructions to play it safe and run out the clock. The quarterback
came into the huddle and said, "The coach says we should play it safe,
but that's what the other team is expecting. Let's give them a surprise."
So he called a pass play. He dropped back and threw, and the defend-
ing cornerback, a spring champion, knifed in, intercepted and headed
for a touchdown.

Now if you know anything about Coach Bryant, you know that the
Alabama quarterback had a problem. He had to catch that corner back
or face Coach Bryant. That quarterback was no runner but he took
after that fleet cornerback, ran him down from behind on the five-yard
line and saved the game. After the game the opposing coach came up
to Bear Bryant and said, "What's this business about your quarterback
not being a runner? He ran down my speedster from behind." "Well,"
said Bryant, "your man was running for six points. My man was running for his life."

I recently heard a song on the radio that reflects the same idea.

Here are the words to this great song:
I'm running for my life, running for my life
Running for my life, running for my life

169

If anyone asks you, what's the matter with me…?
Tell them I'm saved, sanctified
Holy Ghost filled, fire baptized
I've got Jesus on my mind
And I'm running for my life.

That is just what I am doing, running for my life. Satan wants to destroy us. He wants to keep us discouraged and beaten down. But when we accept Jesus Christ as our Lord and Savior, then we are called to greatness. We have a job to do for God. We don't have time to be defeated. I'm running for my life with my mind on Jesus. Won't you run with me too?

> *"I'll never forget the day Bear vowed he could run in his bare feet from the railroad depot to Kingsland in half an hour. He made it with a minute or two to spare."*
>
> —Footsie Benton, childhood friend of Bear Bryant

SABBATH

"So God blessed the seventh day and made it holy because on
it God rested from all his work that he had done in creation"
(Genesis 2; 1-3).

As a boy growing up in Alabama I can go back to a time on Sunday
afternoons when Coach Bear Bryant hosted a television show covering
the events from the Crimson Tide football games the day
before...There on the black and white screen was "Bear" with his
Coca-Cola and bowl of Golden Flake potato chips...The deep southern drawl in his voice as he reminisced every detail of every play his
players made. My father and I dared anyone to change the channel ~
much less be in the room when Coach Bear Bryant was talking. I
would then go out and play the same plays I had seen Johnny Musso
run. Then it would be time to go in a clean up and get ready to go to
church.

We have no civil laws today to protect the Lord's Day. In 21st century
America it is a day for business and for organized commercial (as con-
trasted with familial and recreational) sports more than for worship
That means that, if we keep it, we will chose to keep it for God's glory
and our own good. We will keep it, not because the stores are not open
and the baseball and soccer leagues don't play, and not because our
neighbors will sanction our failure to keep the Day, but because we
want to please God. This gives us an opportunity to exercise faith (does
God know best?) and obedience (will we submit to God's will?).

We can make a beginning of Sabbath keeping just by determining that we will on this Day rest from our work and busy lives and will let nothing (absolutely nothing save providential hindrance) keep us from participation in the public gatherings for worship. When we've made a beginning there will be plenty of time, and the right frame of heart and reference. To consider what else we will and will not do to observe the Day the Lord Jesus calls His own.

"I am a little more appreciative of lay preachers. My mom wanted me to be a preacher."

—Bear Bryant

SEEING ONLY CRIMSON

"He abolished the Jewish law with its commandments, in order to create out of the two races, one new people in union with himself, in this way making peace. By His death on the cross Christ destroyed their enmity; by means of the cross He united both races into one body and brought them back to God." Ephesians 2:15-16

While the University of Alabama and other southern schools had an integrated student body for years, no SEC school had a black athlete on their football team in the early 1970s. Bear Bryant was by no means a racist, but simply didn't pay much attention issue of integration, mainly because he continued to win with his formula. Well as evidenced by the previous few years, his formula was in need of adjusting. Bryant saw good black Alabama players were moving out of state, then coming back and beating his teams. Bryant knew this was an unfair disadvantage and the trend had to change if he was to continue winning. Bryant was credited with helping to stimulate the integration of southern college football. Within a year, all other SEC schools had black athletes on their roster.

I am puzzled at the number of Blacks who proclaim to be Christians, but their behavior would suggest otherwise. There is much bitterness, resentment. and envy in the Black community. These attitudes are choking the progress of Blacks like wild weeds that choke an unkempt garden. The righteousness or evilness of a person is not determined by his race. The Bible is the best book written when it comes to racial harmony—despite the beliefs of the kkk. The Bible says all men have fallen short—not just the white man. It says ye shall know them by their fruits—not their color. It says do not be unequally yoked. This refers to man's spirit—not his race. It says man cannot worship two masters—either God is your Master or your color is your master. We all have been given a gift and it is not our color because even a rock has color. Let the battle trumpets blow. Let the entire righteous people band together and fight our common enemy. God's words are the only weapons. The enemy is not the White man. The enemy is every man who is ignorant—Black, White, and In Between.

"Teamwork—oneness as I like to call it. I don't think there has ever been a self-made man. I think it takes a team."

—Bear Bryant

SLEEVELESS RELIGION

○ ○

"And when you pray, do not be like the hypocrites: for they
love to pray standing in the churches and on the street corners, that they might be seen by men. I say to you, they have
their reward. But when you pray, go into private; pray to
God, which is in secret; and your God who sees in secret will
reward you openly." Mathew 6:5-6.

Bear Bryant was a man who worked hard and played hard, enjoyed life
to it's fullest, and more surprising to a lot of folks, he was a religious
man and compassionate man. When Bear would sit down to a meal he
would bow his head and say grace. He did it that way all the time. He
thought his religion was important and sometimes talked about it in
private quarters. He just didn't wear it on his sleeve for everyone to see.
Behind the tough shell there was a warm and compassionate man with
a tender heart.

Louis Goolsby, Bear's sister, said that they had good Christian parents who taught them to love God. From them they got an apprecia-
tion of faith that helped them all through life.

What was the way and practice of the hypocrites? In all their exer-
cises of devotion, it was plain; the chief thing they aimed at was to be
commended by their neighbors, and thereby to make an interest for
themselves.

What the places were which they chose for their devotions; they
prayed in the synagogues, which were indeed proper places for public
prayer, but not for personal. They pretended hereby to do honor to the
place of their assemblies, but intended to do honor to themselves. They

prayed in the corners of the streets, the broad streets (so the word signifies), which were most frequented. They withdrew thither, as if they
were under a pious impulse, which would not admit delay, but really it
was to cause them to be taken notice of. There, where two streets met,
they were not only within view of both, but every passenger turning
close upon them would observe them, and hear what they said.

The Pharisees had their reward before all the town, and it was a
mere flash and shadow; true Christians shall have theirs before all the
world, angels and men, and it shall be a weight of glory.

"Never be too proud to get down on your knees and pray."

—Bear Bryant

SMELLING ROSES

○ ○

"For all flesh is as grass and all the glory of man as the flower of grass. The grass withers and the flower falls away. But the word of the Lord endures forever. And this is the word which by the gospel is preached to you." 1 Peter 1:24-25.

While Alabama didn't win any national titles during Bryant's playing days, the Tide was one tough team to beat. In 1933 and 1934 Alabama captured the first two SEC Championships and in 1935, upset a very good Stanford team in the Rose Bowl. Known as a tough player, great blocker, and solid catcher, Bryant was selected second-team All-SEC his senior year.

Due to the dominance of Alabama in the Rose Bowl, they decided to limit the participants to only the champion of the Big Ten and the Pacific Ten. Thus to guarantee a chance for the west coast to have a champion.

In Biblical times the emphasis was on aromatic flowers, and it is their fragrance, which is emphasized.

Actually, the use of flowers for decorative purposes is a relatively modern idea. From Biblical times all the way up to and including the Middle Ages, the main use for flowers was for their fragrance. Well, we will try to put things rather delicately. Let's face it, people in Biblical times did not bathe as often as we do today. In fact, they rarely bathed at all. Anything as sweet-smelling as a flower was quite a welcome contrast to the day-to-day odors one usually encountered in ancient times.

The picking of flowers is referred to in the Bible only once: "My beloved has gone to his garden, to the beds of spices, to feed in the gardens, and to gather lilies (Song of Songs 6:2).

"People ask me if I remember anything about the 1935 Rose Bowl and I tell them I remember everything about it."

—Bear Bryant

SNAKE

○ ○
"Which of you, if his son asks for bread, will give him a stone? Or if he asks for a fish, will give him a snake?" Matthew 7:9-10

Kenny "Snake" Stabler, earned his nick-name as an eighth-grader on the junior varsity team of Foley High School, when he zigzagged across the field during a punt return. "A kid said that I ran like a snake," Stabler said. "The coach picked up on it, and it stuck."

In 1964 encouraged by the Legendary Paul "Bear" Bryant, Stabler signed on with the Crimson Tide. Coach Bryant considered him to be one of the best quarterbacks to ever play the game of football.

Voted as "Quarterback of the Century" at the University of Alabama, Stabler was also a member of the 1965 National Championship team. He quarterbacked the 1966 team to an undefeated 11-0 season, and the 1967 squad went 8-1-1. These Tide teams captured two SEC titles and won two of three bowl games, the Orange Bowl and the Sugar Bowl during the Stabler era. They compiled an overall record of 28-3-2.

As I returned home from church, I saw a snake come crawling out of the grass on the side of the road. I figured I'd run over it, if I got there quick enough. And, as I rolled over the snake, I felt the crunch, and looked back to see it rolling up in a ball, wiggling for life. Every time I have a chance, I'll run over a snake, because all kinds are poisonous to me! The enemy is out there, 'crawling out of the bushes', to prey on unsuspecting people. If you aren't 'armed', he will attack you, and it might not be very pleasant. You may live, but you may suffer. But, if we, as Christians, would go after the enemy the way most of us go after a snake, he would be eradicated quickly! The enemy is out to 'kill, steal, and destroy', and we need to be prepared with the correct armor! Most of us are slack in that area of our lives. We will be prepared at times, and, at other times, we don't have a chance. And, don't think the enemy isn't watching you, ready to pounce on you like a flea on a dog! And, he means business. He will hound and hound, until he has you down. But, if you will get in the Word, give God His time in your life, you will find that the enemy will begin to leave you alone, because you are no longer an easy prey. Oh, he won't completely leave you alone, but you can be prepared, when he does strike!

> *"I am thankful he grabbed me by the back of the shirt, yanked me up, shoved me back, got my shoulders straight and refused to let me throw away a great opportunity."*
>
> —Kenny Stabler

STEALING

Despite attempts to smear Bear Bryant's reputation, Alabama won its seventh National Championship in 1964 with Namath at the helm. The Tide repeated as National Champions again in 1965, behind quarterback Steve Sloan. Ken Stabler succeeded him in 1966, but the undefeated Crimson Tide lost the national crown to a Notre Dame team with an inferior record.

Notre Dame claimed the 1966 title despite tying Michigan State, a 4-point underdog. Notre Dame, despite its claim to be a Catholic Christian school, claimed the rightful national championship that was won by Alabama. It had stolen the birthright of Bear Bryant.

The pagans of the wicked world are filled with the lust of greed and think nothing of robbing, stealing, or cheating to get what they want. (How they got something is not important—that they DO have possession of it is all that counts in their book!) But, God's People are not to be that way (for thievery is of the Devil—John 10:10). And we are to respect the rights and privileges given by God to certain people to hold securely the possessions, property, and rights that they do by God's Law.

"Alabama was the victim of some degree of poll bias by the sanctimonious northern press"

—Bud Collins, Boston Globe

SUCCESSION

o o o o o o o o o o o o o o o o o o o o o o o o o o o o o o

"And now, behold, the king walked before you: and I am old and gray headed; and, behold, my sons are with you: and I have walked before you from my childhood unto this day." 1 Samuel 12:2

A young quarterback from Pennsylvania, Joe Namath, was impressed with Bryant's reputation and decided to sign with the Crimson Tide in 1962. Namath succeeded Trammel and would soon become the most famous player to play at the Capstone. Namath threw three touchdown passes in his first game, a 35-0 lashing of Georgia, but the game would become more famous as the subject of a 1963 Saturday Evening Post article charging Bryant and Georgia AD Wally Butts had conspired to "fix" the game.

"When you take a new office," a leader advised, "begin preparing to leave." Leaving? another one wondered. "How can I prepare to leave when I have hardly started living!"? When it was time for him to leave, Samuel was ready, unlike some church leaders who are not only reluctant to leave but do not adequately prepare successors. The poor handing over process in such institutions is reflected in subsequent years. Samuel even accepted evaluation and was ready to take responsibility for any failures. This is a mark of great leadership. But rather than retire honorably, most African politicians wait till they are toppled or felled by bullets.

"Over the years I've learned a lot about coaching staffs and the one piece of advice I would pass on to a young head coach—or a cor-

poration executive or even a bank president—is this: Don't make them in your image."

—Bear Bryant

THE PROGRAM

"A man's heart plans his way; but the Lord programs his steps." Proverbs 16:9

You could argue that Alabama isn't just the program of the century in the SEC, but in all of college football. The Crimson Tide claims 12 national championships. It has played and won more bowl games than any college team. It has won 21 SEC championships, eight more than any other team. You can thank "Bear" Bryant for much of the Crimson Tide's success.

We are more likely to follow God's program when we truly understand:

God's Heart: He is full of compassion and completely just and therefore detests oppression. From the beginning God directed His people toward a more equitable living. In the Old Testament we read of specific programs He instituted as a check and balance system to keep the rich from getting too rich at the expense of others—Year of Jubilee (Lev. 25:8-55), the Sabbatical Year (Lev. 25:1-7), the Law of Tithing (Deut. 14:28-29) and Gleaning (Deut. 24:19-22).

God's Ownership: All things belong to God so we ought not to hold on too tightly. We should, instead, participate with God in meeting people's needs with resources that in reality belong to Him and not us.

According to Luke 4:18-19, Jesus' mission was to free the oppressed and heal the blind. He wanted to see changed lives as a result of His help. Jesus had a balance between meeting physical and spiritual needs. He met physical needs but He also preached and taught truth (Matt. 4:23).

"Bear Bryant was a man in charge of the programs he led and the people he hired to assist him."

—Al Browning, sportswriter

TOWER

"I'd go to Tuscaloosa to watch practice," Bowden said. "I'd get the
guys he didn't want any more. He'd give me a typed list. He'd say,
'Bobby, here's 11 you can have, and if you like, I'll call them in and
recommend that they go play for Howard.' " He'll never forget those
Alabama practices. When Bryant came down from his tower on the
practice field, quicker than a firefighter down the pole, Bowden dived
for cover like everyone else. "I'd be standing there and I'd hear someone say, 'Look out, here he comes,' " Bowden said. "And Bear'd be
coming down that tower. 'Look out, here he comes.' I'll never forget
that as long as I live. "He'd take players on physically and show 'em
how to do a drill. He went pretty dang hard on them. 'Hey, Boy, get
down here,' he'd say. 'Get down here. Charge me! Get after me!' "
Bowden smiled. That was Bear.

In 1998, Senate Special Committee on Y2K chair Senator Robert
Bennett reported, "One of the experts said to me, 'The one thing we
know for sure about this is that we have no historical precedent to
guide us, to tell us what we can expect.'

"Yet when I made that comment to a friend of mine, he said, 'No,
Bob, that's not true. We have a historic example.'

"I said, 'What is it?'

"He said, 'the Tower of Babel. The people got together and decided they were going to build a tower to heaven, and God didn't like it, so he fixed it so they could not talk to each other and that ended it.' "

In the Babel civilization, men sought to define themselves and their world apart from God. God said, "I don't think so."

Men in those days feared being scattered. God scattered them. They dreamed of perpetual unity. God divided them. They confessed with one tongue the glories of man and the works of man's hand. God gave mankind a multitude of languages. The society of Babel disappeared. Such is the fate of every New World Order that challenges the kingdom of God.

> *"A lot has been made about me and the tower. I could just see better up high."*
>
> —Bear Bryant

TRIBUTE

o o o o o o o o o o o o o o o o o o o o o o o o o o o o o o
"Let the elders that rule well be counted worthy of double tribute, especially those who labor in the word and doctrine."
1 Timothy 5:17

Homemade banners hung from the overpasses. Near Bessemer, construction workers in hard hats held up a message scrawled in green paint: "Bear, We Love You and We'll Miss You." Mourners included dozens of Bryant's former players and coaches, along with other famous coaches like Woody Hayes, Frank Broyles, Bobby Dodd, Darrell Royal, John McKay, Eddie Robinson, Duffy Daugherty, Vince Dooley and George Allen. Eight players from Bryant's last team carried the coffin to the gravesite. Tributes from both the meek and the famous filled the columns of newspapers nationwide.

2000 years ago, a Man who changed the course of history lived on earth. Our modern calendar starts from his birth, and his birthday broke history and time countdown in two parts—before and after the birth of Christ.

Who was this Man who lived the most prominent and remarkable life in history? His name is Jesus. The sample of his life has become a source of inspiration for the greatest artists, musicians, and writers of the world. Nowadays, as well as in the past, <u>world leaders, and influential people</u> from all social strata continue to give tribute and honor to the Man named Jesus.

"He was a one of a kind person, which certainly separates him from the masses."

—John Forney, Alabama broadcaster

TURN THE OTHER CHEEK

"But I say unto you, that ye resist not evil: but whosoever shall smite thee on thy right cheek, turn to him the other also." Matthew 5:39

Wally Butts was the athletic director of the University of Georgia in 1962, and worked for the private Georgia Athletic Association, a private corporation, so he was a private citizen. The Saturday Evening Post ran a story that said he conspired to fix a football game between Georgia and Alabama in 1962. Story said an Atlanta insurance salesman had overheard Butts giving Georgia's offensive strategy to Bear Bryant, coach of the Alabama team. Butts sued for $5 million in compensatory damages and $5 million in punitive damages. Jury awarded $60,000 on the first count and $3 million on the second, later reduced to $460,000. Curtis Publishing Co., publisher of The Saturday Evening Post, and the AP appealed to the Supreme Court. Butts won his appeal. Court said Post editors "recognized the need for a thorough investigation of the serious charges" but failed to make the investigation.

We've been assuming that turning the other cheek is another such example because somewhere in our distant past we decided that it delivers this message: "OW! That hurt! But it's safe to hit me again, because I'm a coward and I'm so scared of you! Here, I'll even turn my other cheek toward you so it's more convenient for you to hit me!" I suggest to you that that was a mistake and that turning the other cheek is intended to deliver this very different message:"Please notice—I am not afraid of you at all."This is no cowardly message! On the contrary, it's strong and serene and confident and unafraid. We have been mis-understanding, all along, in spite of the fact that we trust God not to be perverse, and in spite of the fact that nowhere is there any evidence that Jesus was a coward. The misunderstanding has become so embed-ded in our culture and our minds, by habit and repetition that it has hidden the true meaning from us all alongTo turn the other cheek to the one who strikes us with the message that "I am not afraid of you at all," we have to mean it. We can't just pretend. We have to have the serenity and the confidence and the courage that make the message true. We have to know that no matter what happens, we do have the resources and skills necessary to deal with it—so that we have no rea-son to be afraid. Otherwise, we won't be able to follow through.

"A real injustice has been done to the integrity and character not only to myself but to the University of Alabama."

—Bear Bryant on the Saturday Evening Post lies.

UNIFORMS

o o o o o o o o o o o o o o o o o o o o o o o o o o o o o o o
"She is not afraid of the snow for her household, for all her household are clothed with crimson." Proverbs 31:21

Bear Bryant didn't miss a trick. Those tearaway jerseys in the seventies are good example. Alabama was behind against LSU in Birmingham in 1970, Johnny Musso was about to score what would have been the winning touchdown when an LSU player grabbed him by the jersey at the three-yard line and spun him around and tackled him. Alabama ended up losing,14-9, and the Crimson Tide had tearaway jerseys the next week. Alabama went through a lot of them the next few years before the NCAA ruled them out because they were expensive and all the other schools couldn't afford them

There have been a number of studies that indicate our behavior is affected by our attire. This is probably in part why prep schools have a dress code and school uniforms, and why many public schools are turning to uniforms as a way of influencing behavior. Growing up when I did we had three different types of clothes: play clothes, school clothes, and Sunday clothes. The play clothes were for roughhousing and basically getting dirty. Sunday clothes were for our best behavior. When we put them on we behaved differently. We also ate differently. Usually we wore these clothes for celebrations and feasts, weddings, funerals, parties, baptisms. Mostly these clothes were our best as a sign of our love for the Lord. They were an outward representation of an inner reality. Paul says; "let us conduct ourselves becomingly as in the day…" that is the day of the Lord. A bride and groom often wear white as a show of their inner purity. Our behavior should reflect our relationship with the Lord Jesus Christ. Every day is a festival to the Lord by our behavior. What uniform are you wearing today?

"He covered for me and ordered new uniforms."

—Bear Bryant, on his cleaning company ruining Coach Crisp's new uniforms.

UNION

"That which you have seen and heard declare we unto you, that you also may have union with us; and truly our union is with the father, and with his son Jesus Christ." 1 John 1:3

Union was the first coaching post for the legendary Paul W. "Bear" Bryant. In 1936, Bryant came to Union as assistant to A.B. Hollingsworth. After getting his coaching feet wet in Jackson, Bryant went on to become one of the winningest football coaches in history at the University of Alabama. Just two years before Bryant, the Union football team clobbered the University of Mexico in Mexico City with a score of 32-6. The game drew 10,000 spectators.

Foundational to the Christian faith is a clear understanding of our mystical or spiritual union with Jesus Christ

Many Christians live with unhealthy fears and anxieties because they lack an understanding of their spiritual identity in their union with Christ. Therefore, the Holy Spirit desires to illumine our hearts and minds in order that we might move from an insecure position to a secure position in our relationship with God and people.

One mistake quite often is made by speaking of a time in which we made a commitment to Christ, rather than when Christ made a commitment to us. Scripture says that God chose us "in Him" before the foundation of the World.

God, who is omniscient and omnipotent, causes us to discover in time what has been determined in eternity, or before time began. In the fullest biblical sense, our union with Christ began in eternity past and goes through time into eternity future. The Spirit of Truth through the written Word confirms this by the assurance that, "He who has begun a good work in you will complete it until the day of Jesus Christ".

In summary, Father God knows that we come from the womb spiritually dead. We all develop fears and insecurities to some degree. He wants us to know that we are special because we were chosen "in Christ" before the foundation of the world was framed and by His Holy Spirit and Word, He will renew our minds and build a divine confidence of our union with Christ.

> *"The Union coach didn't come to practice very often so I had my own way. The only bad thing was they didn't pay me on time"*
>
> —Bear Bryant

VICTORY

o o o o o o o o o o o o o o o o o o o o o o o o o o o o o o o
"The victor: I will give him the right to sit with Me on My
throne, just as I also won the victory and sat down with My
Father on His throne. "Revelations 3:21

The list of honors stretches on and on and on for Bear Bryant. It bog-
gles the mind, looking at it all at once now. But at the time Bryant was
piling up the records, his winning came to be expected, even taken for
granted. The wins were news, but rarely surprising news. That was just
how things were supposed to be. After all, he was Coach Bryant, and
none who knew him was ever surprised by a Bryant victory—only by a
Bryant defeat. It is difficult to imagine anyone ever again weathering
the pressures of college football long enough to accomplish even half of
what Bryant did. It is even more difficult to imagine anyone devoting
the time and energy to football that he did. If a young coach starting
out today with an eye on Bryant's won-lost record alone (323-85-17)
would have to survive as a head coach 32 seasons and average 10 wins a
year just to get close. The records tell only a small part of the near epic
Bear Bryant story.

About what you do after you achieve victory. If you win, if you
overcome adversity, if you defeat an opponent, do you praise God or
relish in self? Do you see who brings the blessings of victory in life or
do you give yourself credit? Winning can inflate the ego and build up
the self. Winning can kill humility. Who gets credit? The Lord sup-
plies us with abundant resources to do His will in every circumstance.
The Lord gives us the ability to win out over incredible odds. When we
win out, instead of giving ourselves credit or relishing the power we

have, we need to come to our Lord on our knees in contrite humility. When we win, we must look to our Lord who gives us our abilities, our opportunities, and our resources. It is from God that all victories and blessings flow, and not from us.

"Winning isn't everything, but it sure beats anything that comes in second.'

—Bear Bryant

VOICE OF GOD

o o o o o o o o o o o o o o o o o o o o o o o o o o o o o
"And when he putts forth his own sheep, he goes before
them, and the sheep follow him: for they know his voice."
John 10:4

Bear Bryant almost never mis-spoke. He knew or seemed to visualize as
he was speaking, how what he was saying would. Look in print or
sound on radio or television. He had a certain charisma-a presence.
Wherever he went—a pep rally, a meeting or wherever he walked into
a room, when he spoke, every eye and every ear was tuned in to him.

When you are listening for God's voice, how do you know that He
is the one speaking? Are you hearing some other voice? People say, "I
am asking the Lord for direction in my life, but it's like I'm hearing
two different voices. How do I know that God is the one who is speaking to me, or if Satan is telling me this? Or am I just talking to myself?"

Jesus says, "My sheep hear My voice and I know them and they follow Me". Identifying God's voice should be the normal, natural walk
of the Spirit-filled, committed believer. But the newborn lamb would
not necessarily know the shepherd's voice. A sheep that has been there
for a while would know the shepherd's voice. As you are praying and
seeking the Lord's mind, you will know that you have heard His
voice—not an audible voice, but the Spirit of God speaking to you.
God speaks to us so that we may understand truth. He speaks primarily
through His Word, through the Holy Spirit to our consciences,
through circumstances, through other people. By applying what you
hear to the truth of Scripture, you can learn to recognize His voice.
God wants to be our leverage in living, empowering us to feel better

about ourselves, more excited about our future, more grateful for those we love and more enthusiastic about our faith. If you are a believer in Jesus Christ, God has given you His Holy Spirit to help you live life according to His perfect plan.

> *"Since coming back to Alabama Paul Bryant has led us alumni and fans down a royal road to gridiron riches. Along the way he has become a legend, and none of us who made the journey will ever forget it or be able to show our true appreciation for this man."*

> —John Forney—Voice of Alabama

WALKING ON WATER

○ ○

"And he said, Come. And when Peter was come down out of the ship, he walked on the water, to go to Jesus." Matthew 14:29

Bear Bryant and the Tiger Coach were fishing...Tiger coach asked, "Is it really true that you can walk on water?" Bear Bryant, said, "Of course I can walk on water." Tiger Coach asked him to demonstrate. Bear Bryant stepped off the side of the boat into the water...he went down.... Tiger Coach, feeling bad, pulled him into the boat.... Bear Bryant said "thanks" but asked that he not tell the Alabama people that he couldn't walk on water.... Tiger Coach said, I won't tell the Bama people that you can't walk on water, if you won't tell that I pulled you out!!!

Walking on water is easy to someone with impulsive boldness, but walking on dry land as a disciple of Jesus Christ is something altogether different. Peter walked on the water to go to Jesus, but he "followed Him at a distance" on dry land We do not need the grace of God to withstand crises—human nature and pride are sufficient for us to face the stress and strain magnificently. But it does require the supernatural grace of God to live twenty-four hours of every day as a saint, going through drudgery, and living an ordinary, unnoticed, and ignored existence as a disciple of Jesus. It is ingrained in us that we have to do exceptional things for God? But we do not. We have to be exceptional in the ordinary things of life, and holy on the ordinary streets, among ordinary people? and this is not learned in five minutes.

You can't walk on water. It won't support your weight. In reality, Peter was walking on the Word of Jesus. Jesus told Peter, "Come," and that one word, spoken by the Creator Himself, had enough power to enable Peter to walk on water. Peter wasn't just walking on water; he was walking on God's Word. The Word of God is surer than anything physical that we see around us. In Peter's case, that meant getting out of the boat and walking on the water. He couldn't have stayed in the boat and said, "I'm trusting you Jesus. I'm acting on your word." He had to do what Jesus said to do. It's the same with us. If you really trust Jesus, then do what He tells you to do. Don't listen to the guys in the boat. It would have been crazy for them to get out of the boat. They weren't the ones the Lord told to, "come." You must have a word to stand on that is from God.

"Sometimes the wagon would actually float across the creek, I was amazed that the mules could swim so well."

—Bear Bryant

WISHBONE

o o o o o o o o o o o o o o o o o o o o o o o o o o o o o o
"We wish to see Jesus." John 12:21

1971 would be a turning point for Alabama and Bryant in more ways than one. First, Bryant was credited with helping to stimulate the integration of southern college football, by recruiting Alabama's first black player. Second, Bryant would engineer an offensive change from the pro-attack to the wishbone, thus setting in place a dominance of the 70's.

The scene was fresh in Phil's mind. His uncle, after chewing the last bit of turkey off a wishbone, pointed it at him and stated, "Christians are just a bunch of narrow-minded hypocrites. With this thought, Phil sank back in the pew. The preacher said, "Christ is the way, the truth, and the life." His thoughts shot back to his uncle, waiving a wishbone in the air. Their way can't be the only way," he reassured himself. Phil left that day holding on to a wishbone of his own.

Phil grew proud of his wishbone over the years. Under the banner of open-mindedness and intellectualism, Phil waived his wishbone in the air every chance he got. Phil crawled into bed one win night and woke up just outside the gates of heaven. An angel greeted Phil. He cried out, "Angel what must I do to enter the city? The angel opened up a large book. "Please, please, please tell me it's in there." Phil rubbed his eyes. His name was not in the book. Suddenly the gates swung open. Phil slid his hand into his pocket and grabbed the wishbone. A human shadow filled the open gap. "Ahh, who are you?" Phil asked. The man opened his hands up toward Phil. "Oh, why it's you, Jesus." Christ responded, "I never knew you." "Oh, Jesus. Please, please let me pass! I did not know." Jesus responded, "Yes you did. Remember the church? Remember my plea? You heard but you refused to listen. I'm the key to the gate behind me." "But Jesus, I did not want to be narrow-minded. You see, I've carried around this wishbone all these years and." Jesus shook his head back and forth, compassionately. "My wishbone, Jesus? Can't I use my wishbone?" Jesus stepped behind the gate. Phil raised the wishbone in the air. Jesus pulled the gate shut. Phil pulled on his wishbone. The bone began to crack. A loud voice boomed, "Depart from me. I never knew you!" A sulfur smell surrounded Phil. Clamoring for the gate, he slid back into the darkness.

> *There is a lot we don't know about the wishbone, but it is the best formation I have seen."*
>
> —Bear Bryant

WRESTLING

o o o o o o o o o o o o o o o o o o o o o o o o o o o o o o o o

"And Jacob was left alone; and there wrestled a man with him until the breaking of the day. And when he saw that he prevailed not against him, he touched the hollow of his thigh; and the hollow of Jacob's thigh was out of joint, as he wrestled with him. And he said, Let me go, for the day breaketh. And he said, I will not let thee go, except thou bless me. And he said unto him, What is thy name? And he said, Jacob. And he said, Thy name shall be called no more Jacob, but Israel: for as a prince hast thou power with God and with men, and hast prevailed. And Jacob asked him, and said, Tell me, I pray thee, thy name. And he said, Wherefore is it that thou dost ask after my name? And he blessed him there. And Jacob called the name of the place Peniel: for I have seen God face to face, and my life is preserved." Genesis 32:24-30.

Years of hard work left Bryant strong and it seems a little hard-headed. One day, a man in a covered wagon came to Fordyce offering a dollar a minute to anyone who would wrestle a bear. Young Paul jumped at the chance. A dollar a minute was far better than picking cotton all day for 50 cents. Bryant entered the ring at the Lyric Theater and quickly charged the bear. He quickly got the animal in a bear hug. Quickly it broke free of its muzzle and bit Paul on the ear. Bryant saw blood and ran screaming from the theater. The man skipped town before Paul could collect his money, but he did earn a nickname. From that day forward, he would be known as "Bear" Bryant.

God didn't get mad at Jacob or kill him. Instead, God was very close to Jacob during the struggle and even ended up blessing him. The greatest blessing that God gave Jacob came many years later. Jesus Christ was born into Jacob's family. And because of Jesus, Jacob could have eternal life. And so can we. Like Jacob, we don't have to be afraid to wrestle with God. God doesn't get mad at us when we question Him or when we struggle with the way things are\ going in our lives. If we don't give up, and if we stay close to God, He will stay close to us. He will use our problems and questions to give us a blessing. Can you think of any ways God could use our problems and questions to bless us?˙How would you answer the person who asked, "Is it wrong for me to wrestle with God?"

"So this must be what God looks like."

—George Blanda when he first saw Bear.

THE FIRST CHURCH OF
THE BEAR

Long before I knew what a University was…I knew there was Alabama football. Long before I knew that engineers were more than train conductors…I knew there was Alabama football.

My first words as a child were "Roll Tide." Although I don't remember the experience myself, I'm sure that I ripped my pacifier from my mouth and with wild eyes, flaring nostrils and clenched fists, proclaimed it with the most fervor my baby gibberish would allow.

Although I began to follow Bama long during the Bear's era, I understand that the quote "I ain't never been nothing but a winner," when grumbled over the loud speakers at Bryant Denny, carries more meaning than simply remembering a coach's legacy.

Those words capture the essence of Alabama football. Can you name one other football program that wouldn't publicly crucify its mascot at halftime to have half the tradition that Alabama football has right now, even under NCAA sanctions? Bama's never been nothing but a winner, sanctioned or not.

It has been a tradition at Bryant Denney Stadium to play a pre-game video featuring video clips of Alabama's 12 national championships (that's TWELVE, not SIX, for the folks at ESPN), and more importantly, Paul "Bear" Bryant and his words of wisdom. Some even compared the voice of The Bear to the voice of God.

In light of this tradition to go so far as to deify one of the greatest college football coaches in history, I believe I have come up with the basis of a new religion that might someday grace the Capstone. I introduce to you "The First Church of The Bear."

The church shall not discriminate on the basis of age, gender, race, national origin or sexual orientation. All people can become members, granted they pledge their devotion to the church through demonstrating devotion at each service and obeying the commandments of the church:

1. Thou shalt have no other college teams before the Crimson Tide.

2. Thou shalt not take the name of The Bear in vain.

3. Remember the Game Day and keep it holy.

4. Honor thy forefathers and thy current leaders of Crimson Tide football.

5. Thou shalt not kill, even in the name of the Crimson Tide.

6. Thou shalt not betray the Crimson Tide, or the holy word of The Bear.

7. Thou shalt not steal, except to dishonor Auburn or Tennessee.

8. Thou shalt not bear false witness to an outstanding Tide play.

9. Thou shalt not covet another team's players.

10. Thou shalt not covet another team's apparel.

Services are held at every Alabama home game in Bryant-Denny Stadium. Church members are encouraged, but not required, to attend services at Legion Field. Service times vary due to television coverage.

Attendance at services is spiritually necessary, although home worship during Birmingham home games or away games or for those who cannot attend services is allowed.

The required dress for services is not formal. Clothing colors must be crimson, white or both. Body paint of those colors is also acceptable.

Showing "the spirit" during service is not only allowed, but also encouraged.

Indulgences are not necessary, even for small sins against the church, such as doubting the Crimson Tide when it plays a well-regarded (or overrated) team. Donations to the church are welcome, and may be rewarded by better seats in the church. Major sins against the church, such as committing actions that bring NCAA violations to the football program, are grounds for excommunication.

When the voice of "God," a.k.a. The Bear, is broadcast over the loudspeakers, members are encouraged to cheer reverently.

Collection shall be taken with houndstooth hats being passed around each section of the stadium. The love offerings collected will be put into a building fund for such improvements as placing stained-glass windows in the four corners of the stadium. The windows would be based on the artwork of Daniel A. Moore, depicting "The Goal Line Stand," "The Kick," "The Sack" and "The Third Saturday Classic."

Singing and chanting along with the congregation is strongly encouraged, but singing talent is not required.

Communion shall consist of Golden Flake potato chips and Coca-Cola. Um, I mean, Pepsi. Jack Daniels in your Pepsi is optional.

Past Crimson Tide players are eligible for canonization. Current Tide players become eligible their senior year, though a strong St. Brodie movement may be grounds to skirt the rules and commence canonization.

Dancing is allowed in the church. Drinking in moderation is also allowed. Throwing objects onto the field, such as cups, is not allowed, unless one is throwing them at blasphemers of the church, such as opposing cheerleaders.

If the church sounds good to you, I invite you to join. You don't even have to leave your current religion to become a member. I hope to see many new members.

Remember, if you talk to people who didn't go to the game, just assume they sold their tickets and held their own service at home. Goodbye, and Bear bless.

0-595-25599-X

Printed in the United States
127275LV00006B/1-18/A